ROGER TALLON

this series edited by
PIERRE STAUDENMEYER

ROGER TALLON

GILLES DE BURE

CHLOÉ BRAUNSTEIN

CONTENTS

Like a plane without wings

*I*n 1971, the users of the SNCF discovered a new object, the extent to which it was revolutionary barely remembered today: the Corail train.

Information at the entrance of carriages, time-tables, map… at first glance the tone was set. The means of communication became likewise the support for information. Inside, an open space, all soft and round, eliminated the sacrosanct compartments and made the train resemble an airplane. Perhaps only the dominating orange and brown were sacrificed to fashion at the start of the 70s. Thus, a railway revolution. And, like all revolutions, a painful birth. Because the world of rail had not spared its hostility on the programme perfected by Tallon. Disruption of habits, rocking the image, comfort of passengers, all elements calculated to ruffle a profession entrapped in its corporatism. A little while later, Tallon paid for his advanced vision by seeing his project for the TGV Sud-Est (Paris-Lyon) refused. But he would have his revenge in 1983 with the TGV Atlantique and would impose, from that time on, his idea of public transport. One after another, the TGV North-American (Canada and Texas), the mega-TGV (the Duplex) and the TGV Eurostar would bear his stamp. As already, the Mexico subway, the Matra 208, and the funicular at Montmatre, and the Meteor…

Would Roger Tallon only be the man of a single space, the designer of all the trains, the man of the railway? Certainly not. Throughout the world he is considered today as the most complete French designer. Though celebrated, honored, recognized, he still remains almost unknown to the wider public. The truth is that this young man of seventy has not conformed to the mediatization of design that started at the beginning of the 80s. And yet, he has everything to seduce the media: laughing eyes, vigorous walk, animated gestures, commanding, rapid-fire voice, almost fifty years of conceiving, drawing and realizing machine tools and seats, televisions and staircases, lamps, watches and ski-boots, fridges and multiple telecommunication units…

"I work for others and to very precise programmes. It doesn't interest me to stamp my products; I leave that to the stylists. Design is form without fundamental segregation. Play, humour, fantasy and eroticism are not forbidden here," he stated in 1969. A way of saying that, for him, what counts above all is to create a product both simple and complex, legible, easy to access: "The length of the instructions is inversely proportional to a good conception of the product," added, sarcastically, the one who ignores none of the modes of existence of techniques, objects, systems and networks.

The devastating humour of Tallon has no limit. It hits head on technicians unsure of their knowledge, businesses jammed in their certainties, leaders seated on their habits, colleagues planted before

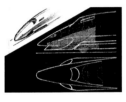

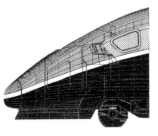

Three generations of TGV: 001, 1967 - Atlantic, 1973 - Duplex, 1996
Aerodynamic research for the TGV 400, 1999

their psyches, journalists and other media people blinded by all that shines… A funny but not an easy man!

In a state of permanent curiosity, he's had a good thirty-five years of teaching and educational research at the Applied Arts, the Art Décos, in the Institutes of the Environment and the commissions of the ICSID (International Council of Societies of Industrial Design): "I teach to learn," he slipped in, bursting with laughter. His credo in the matter: give to students the taste of extraordinary things so they will be successful in pushing at the limits of ordinary things.

Everywhere Roger Tallon is called "Mister TGV". To limit him to that territory and one fails to appreciate him. His artist friends, among others, bear witness. Where would be the fire paintings or architectures of air by Yves Klein, the expansions of César, the qualification of quantity by Arman, without that small push from Tallon?

How is it then that that inspired Jack-of-all-trades is so little known? Is it his discretion, his refusal to play social games or activities of such mundanity? And yet Tallon has explored everything, experimented with everything, opened so many doors through which so many people have surged.

At the same time, Zeus, Janus and Shiva, Tallon is a tree. The one which takes root the deepest and projects the highest. A tree, a cross-roads and a catalyst all at once. The precise spot for the collisions of complexities and paradoxes, eclecticism and ambiguity, humour and rigor, ingenuity and conviction, public silence and private chat, modesty and violence, rectilinear trajectory and constant digressions…

June 1970. The Boeing landed smoothly on the tarmac at Kennedy Airport. Accompanying Tallon, Jean Aubert and Jean Baudrillard, François Barré and Claude Braunstein, Henri Ciriani and some others stepped out. They went to the IBM head office, in the heart of Manhattan, for a reception given in honor of the French guests destined for the International Design Conference in Aspen (IDCA), courtesy of an IBM grant.

Next morning, they flew to Denver, then Aspen. The flight from Denver to Aspen lasted only forty minutes, but presented a "steep climb" of more than 4,000 meters between sheer rock faces and with monstrous air pockets. At disembarkation in Aspen, everybody was shaking. The flight had been so "bumpy" that none had come out of it unscathed. One passenger hadn't responded to the call: Roger Tallon. He sat tight, glued to his seat, his fingers dug into the armrests. After quite a while, he was dragged from the little twin-engine and rejoined the group, wobbling, dazed, his mind elsewhere.

"I was born in the plane age and dreamed of being a pilot. At seven I started to build models: planes and cars. My two heroes were Bournazel and Mermoz, the centaur and archangel," he related, both pensive and amused.

Roger did not become an archangel. It was Bournazel who carried him away, and Tallon rode many machines from motorbike to train, evidently preferring an adherence to terra firma than great arabesques in the open sky.

No wonder, consequently, with such childhood dreams, he counted General Motors and Dupont of Nemours among his first clients, then Sud Aviation and Alsthom, and, later, the SNCF and RATP.

Co-founder of the Jeunesses Musicales de France, close to artists and writers, his mother imagined him a musician, artist, writer. Was it a reaction? The fact remained that Roger devoted himself to techniques. Especially when, in 1937, his father took him to "Expo". There, he had a shock. There, he discovered the future, what tomorrow would be. Since that time, technique, manipulation, mastery would be no more than a means. The future, wild schemes, castles in the air, took first place in his imagination. At the Exposition Universelle in 1937, at the foot of the Eiffel Tower, in the coolness of the pavilions of Nazi Germany and the Soviet Union, both who mistrusted each other, measuring each other before the clash, Roger Tallon discovered the breath and the dream. He was at home, in total complicity, even more so as he confronted himself with his destiny.

So much at home that he returned to the place of the Expo and lived there for more than thirty-five years. Like a looped loop…

The war passed but not military obligations. He was recruited into the "Premier Cuir" in Germany. An illustrious cavalry regiment who were the one of Turenne. But tanks had replaced horses and it was "King Jean," the general de Lattre de Tassigny, who was in command.

Tallon did not stay for long in his "sardine tin". He was pulled out and posted to the Intelligence Service. Congenitally curious, he rejoiced in that move. He placed there, at that precise moment, his apprenticeship to the profession of designer. An officer in the Intelligence Service of the army of occupation in Germany, his job consisted in verifying, confirming, cross-checking information. According to him the essence of design itself.

But what is design for Roger Tallon?

"Design is not characterized by an activity of specific conception, but by the behaviour of the conceiver in the exercise of that activity."

As positivist as he is, Tallon does not avoid the rocks, the dangers, those that consist in defining through the negative. Like God, like humour, design is defined in relation to what it is not. That's not to know well the "celestial acrobat" who added: "Design is a conduct which refuses the un-thought, the hazardous or unexpected solution. It is a search for information and method in the treatment of the problem."

One can see clearly the scheme from that point forth. But what about the sketching as, basically, isn't the best definition of design that half-whimsical: "The sketching of a scheme" (Le dessin d'un dessein.)?

To that, Tallon retorted: "The relationship one has with beauty in our job mustn't be one of aesthetics. In order to free ourselves of it, at one stage we even invented a specific vocabulary. A funny vocabulary which included words like *druft*, *glonf*, *splurd* or *schtrong*. That specific, exclusive, vocabulary allowed us to evoke without naming them, notions like "cut", "sensual", "mechanical brute". It was a sort of affranchisement."

An affranchisement perhaps, but even more another way for Tallon to feed his hunger for words. Tallon is a man who says, a man who speaks, in whatever way he can.

Untitled
Origin of the line for the new SNCF logo, 1985

At that stage of verbality, it is neither impenitence, nor lack of restraint, but well and truly a compulsion. His old accomplice, the Italo-American graphic designer Massimo Vignelli, fascinated by his flow, wrote: "He has an anecdote to tell about each place, about everything that can happen in Paris... his universal knowledge jumps from one subject to another, it's an endless loop that touches every aspect of life."

Another of his supporters, Marianne Persine Heissler, who introduced the design management into the bosom of the SNCF as early as 1969, agreed and added: "That torrent of speech in which met, pell-mell, thick and fast, assumptions allegedly acquired, paradoxical deductions, facts and references coming from a multitude of fields of knowledge—the lot amplifying an unstoppable argumentation—destabilized the listener who quickly lost their footing and let themselves be carried away, flummoxed, like a straw, by that irresistible current."

Tallon presents his projects, proposes his solutions, strikes his convictions like a street trader on the pavement of the Bazar de l'Hôtel de Ville. Understand who can, buy who wants, join who decides...

Yes, that compulsive chatterbox is a torrent. He talks so much that one imagines he's incapable of listening. And yet, what would he have to tell if he was not permanently listening? Simply, his listening is different, as if he was predicting, preceding what the other had to say.

However that may be, to converse with him is equivalent to a permanent fight to seize hold of the microphone. To such an extent in fact that one of his american clients, for whom he had designed printers, had laid down a very strict rule between them. They only saw each other for lunch in a restaurant. And the one who held the salt cellar in his hand had the right to speak. One imagines the scuffles above the table, the spilt glasses, the stained elbows, the farcical laughter, the alarm of the neighboring tables and waiters…

Actually, Shiva suits him better than Zeus or Janus, even if… One imagines him with his six hands in permanent agitation, in constant emulation. Six arms and six hands which relay un-relentingly that box of ideas which throbs frenetically in his skull.

"Even in the night I wake up to jot down an idea… I have more than five hundred plans in a cupboard we call, between ourselves, the *freezer*, for they come out of it sometimes after many many years," he revealed in 1982.

That compulsion, no more verbal but accumulative, struck him as long ago as 1955. At twenty six, an intuition took hold of him: design and the future were the same thing. Thus it was vital to consider everything, absolutely everything, the sound as well as the space, cybernetics as well as food, fundamental research as well as photosynthesis. For five years, the "futuristic period" of Tallon expanded, emerging on the establishment of a "grand reservoir of pure ideas." Five years of trials and errors, discoveries, exploration and unbridled enthusiasm. Then he swung back, passing from listing to casting, from objects to people. But that grand reservoir of pure ideas foreshadowed the *freezer*. Of course, it doesn't look remotely like a fridge, for it is made of big bags in which notes and drawings accumulate, ideas and reflections which from time to time rise, develop, and take shape.

As, for example, in the case of the TS folding chair.

One fine day, Tallon stopped at a red light, scrawled on a pad a vague sketch which fixed the idea he had for a folding chair. On arrival at the agency, the sketch was filed in the *freezer*. A few months later, Sentou wanted to introduce into his collections a new stackable chair and he asked Tallon. Tallon took out his sketch, convinced Sentou that a folding chair was a thousand times better than a stackable and the trick had worked.

Moreover, the chair, of a rare simplicity and obviousness, achieved a real success. As surface treatment, Tallon enjoys playing with uncertainties. But a controlled uncertainty and in perfect adequation with the industrial tool. The opposite of the aleatory seen by Gaetano Pesce who, more of an artist, enjoys perverting the industrial tool.

There is little place for the aleatory in the work of Tallon, who is not particularly attracted by accidental variables. At best, one can consider as unexpected the success of the Téléavia television drawn in 1966, which was for him only an attempt at a do-it-yourself marriage between the only two screens currently available then on the market, the radar screen and the television screen.

Such "misadventure" happened to Ettore Sottsass Jr around the same period, with his "Valentine" typewriter, created for Olivetti. Sottsass treated it with condescension and it earnt an immediate and resounding success.

From both sides of the Alps, Tallon and Sottsass, without realizing it, redefined modernity through two everyday objects that one wouldn't imagine carried so much meaning.

In reality Tallon perceived it perfectly well when he declared: "There is no opposition between rationalism and intuition. The two go hand in hand. The essential is to tidy thought, to fix it is criminal."

Intuition, rationalism, rapidity. For Tallon temporality is written speed. Speed of reaction, speed of execution.

Nothing he likes better than to recount how the funicular of Montmatre had been desired, conceived, decided, developed, realized, and put into service in less than eighteen months. The equivalent of a world record. "Thanks to Christian Blanc who is big game," he added. Tallon likes big game, those great autocratic bosses who take immediate decisions and insist on supersonic results: "For it's there, there with them that design occurs."

For Tallon, everything is a question of opportunity. Opportunity seized, of course. Nothing is important, but everything is essential: "If one connects me up to something, I get passionate and set off." Once again, speed of reaction, simultaneous with speed of perception.

Tallon remembers. In 1956, he conceived a rapid little motorbike and submitted the idea to the Derny Society which made motorized bicycles used for training racing cyclists.

Meeting on a friday, the project captivated. Delighted, Tallon went off to spend the weekend in Brittany. Early on monday morning he was summoned to Derny. The boss had been to Technès on saturday morning, found the plans for the motorbike, taken them away and had them realized during the week-end. The first prototype of the *Taon* was ready, Tallon could try it. Shortly after, on the 25th September, during its presentation on the circuit at Monthléry, it was a great success. At the controls, the designer had transformed into a test pilot and caressed the wind.

When Tallon talks about the TGV, he whispers: "It is metal which flows into space".

Everything is going too fast. Especially Tallon. His collaborators, old and new, complain about it sometimes. For Tallon functions like a racing driver who cannot drive while looking at the road.

Too slow the road, too fast the car. The pilot has the road in his head, behind his eyes. When he takes bend number 5, he is already at number 7. That's how Tallon works. Suddenly he stops in the middle of a sentence, in the middle of a project. Nobody knows why. Nobody understands. But he knows, he is already elsewhere, far ahead.

"Who cares about time, anyway! Even if to be a designer means above all ANTICIPATING. But short, middle, and long terms, they don't exist for me. Especially as everything that is produced could have been produced much earlier, but one is always blocked by a system of thinking. The duration of a product or a system, that's what counts! Anyway, time leaves its mark, even without a date."

Marc Lebailly, Tallon's partner, agreed: "The programmes carried out by Roger don't date. They bear witness to an age."

Curious paradox, formidable ambiguity that the one who forces to witness without dating. Perhaps the solution can be found in that phrase used by Françoise Jollant-Kneebone which tends to define Tallon's activity as a "permanent incompletion".

There again, a paradox. If the work of Tallon is exemplary of what is a culmination, how can it participate in incompletion?

Tallon enjoys those ambiguities and paradoxes, he who prides himself on being a *"problem solver"*, but doesn't like anything more than to maintain the mystery.

"Incompletion? Why not? But I would've preferred the reference to permanent cinema. I liked that age when one could enter the cinema anytime. When one could see the end before the beginning. In a funny sort of way, the film never started, never ended, it was like life. Yes, as to incompletion, I prefer without beginning or end."

"I am a *problematician* for a project is born from an equation. In that I feel closer to Le Corbusier and Charlotte Perriand than the Expressionists. I've never thought that what I do *is* Tallon's," the designer said with candour, before quickly adding: "I like the fact of not knowing the final shape in advance, that that shape could still surprise me."

Right away Tallon refutes all formalism. Another paradox if one considers that, in reality, there is in all his production an obvious rejection of formalism, but that at the same time a constant and very powerful style blazes there. Tallon insists often on the fact that the aesthetics of the object is without reality, that only the intelligence of the object counts. Just as he rejects that reductive definition that every function generates the right form:

"It seems wrong to say that each function determines an ideal form. By creating forty-two different objects issuing from the

Roger Tallon as a child (with the cap on), visiting the International Exhibition on Arts and Techniques in Modern Life, 1937
A view of the exhibition

same form—tables, chairs, lights, signals, mirrors, telephone booths, flower tubs, cutlery, glasses, plates—I prove on the contrary that with one single form one can do many things. It is a sort of deductive functionalism. It consists in declining all the possibilities at all the scales, starting from the same coherent plastic system."

It would then not be the function creating the form, but rather the form, the forms, creating the functions. Nice reversal, as usual from the most paradoxical of speakers.

As contrast, again Françoise Jollant-Kneebone: "Most of the household objects he's created have become great classics, and even if the industrial adventure has been cut short, and they have not been produced, or not many of them anyway, they remain in the collective memory because they are "read", because one grasps the internal logic, and because they impose themselves, in fashion, as evidence."

With his usual rhetorical versatility, Tallon, to whom we owe the advent of the word design in France, to whom we are indebted for a largely shared mistrust towards what belongs to stylism or *styling*, resumed: "I will always try to go beyond that common-place aesthetic in order to reach the level of the style. It is for me, as well as for some others, a profound requirement, for style is the direct expression of the spirit of the period. Style is neither school, nor fashion, nor reminiscence. Style has to be invented facing the problem."

Sometimes, Tallon gets irritated. He's quite happy to be credited with such or such statement, such and such invention or ambition. But sometimes he likes to put things back in place.

"The French milieu tries to force doors open. At one point, design was called "industrial aesthetics". What's the point of gallicizing the name, of practising any linguistic chauvinism? In France, everything has developed in those kinds of successive misunderstandings. Would it occur to you to gallicize the word *jazz*?"

To recall a bistro conversation, at the Lutétia, the Coupole, the Sélect or at Lipp, God knows where... in which Tallon participated, and at which Claude Bolling said: "For design, as for jazz, French people have no tempo."

Almost thirty-five years have elapsed since that remark, and Tallon has had time to punctuate his journey with an infinity of design products.

In retrospect, one finally considers that the non-forms of Tallon compose in reality an ambiguous and indeterminate plastic vocabulary.

"That doesn't look like anything else but reminds me of something," one says each time. "That's familiar to me, but I cannot see how or why."

All that production is at the same time vital and indeterminate, dense and unsettled, immediate and uncertain...

Uniting the whole, a sort of congenital roundness that one finds everywhere, from the Téléavia to the TGV, passing by the Bulle, the Taon, the Cryptogammes, the Lip watch, the Corail, the TS chair, the spiral staircase, the 3T or the SNCF logo... that's to say the same formal vocabulary conveying even more than functions, informations. As if the universe of forms characteristic of Tallon was, finally, nothing but an immense, infinite field of communication.

"I am a man of images. I was born at the same time as talking pictures. My culture, my imaginary world, it's the cinema. I have, by the way, spent my youth in Montreuil, Méliès' town. My neighbor was Mrs Loyal, the widow of the famous Loyal. So cinema, circus… that stirred me! Then Chaplin, Keaton…"

Méliès, Chaplin, Keaton… one thinks of "A Trip to the Moon", "City Lights" or "The General", and one thinks all of that goes well with Tallon. Dream and reality mixed, poetry and technological mastery entangled. Talking about the Veronic camera, Dominique Païni draws a portrait of Tallon, all finesse and depth, undoubtedly because the cinema functions very similarly to Tallon, dream and reality, poetry and industry…

"…to project the appearances of things on the appearances of things. However, his projections of faces on busts, made in 1965, produced an illusionist sensation whose interest exceeded the visual game alone… Tallon displayed a real sharpness in order to question the relation between images and things…." Pushing even further, Païni insists on the capacity of Tallon to demonstrate "his talent as producer of signs rather than of objects."

Most certainly Tallon is a tree which takes root and projects itself. A tree of transmission too, for he has been the starting point, the place of discovery for a great number of people.

June 1967. The telephone rang on the desk of a very young

journalist working for an obscure bimonthly magazine oddly titled *L'Immobilier*.

"A Mr Clouzot for you," the operator announced. The Mr in question wanted to have further information about that strange cardboard furniture on which the young journalist had written his article in the last issue. After having given the information, the journalist inquired about their use. "I'm thinking of using them for the set of my next film." A slight pause, then: "You're Henri-Georges Clouzot?" "Yes." "But how come you have the magazine, do you read it?" "No, but yesterday evening, while having diner with César and Tallon at the Coupole, the conversation turned on my film and its lack of set, and César, who had *L'Immobilier* in his mini-moke, went to fetch it." "What, César reads *L'Immobilier*?" "This is odd, young man, you seem flattered that I'm calling you, astonished that César has your journal, but you don't breathe a word on Tallon!" "Who?" "Roger Tallon, the great French designer." "The great what?" "Designer, you don't know what it is?" "No, to my great regret." "Then, you should meet him!" "You have his phone number?"

Five minutes later, a meeting was arranged with Tallon for two days later at 11 in the morning.

At number 38 Boulevard Raspail, at the back of a courtyard, the offices of Technès were scarcely vibrant.

"I'm yours in a minute," announced a kind of atomic battery mounted on two legs, with short, black hair, and glasses on a chain. A few minutes later: "So, what can I do for you?" "Explain to me what you do. What is design, what is a designer?" "Oh right! I see..."

An hour later, in the middle of a sentence without beginning or end, Tallon abruptly asked "Are you free for lunch? Yes, good, give me one minute." His hand stretched towards the phone, dialed a number, and his voice, all charm, excused himself: "Hello, dear friend. I'm sorry, something turned up, can we postpone our lunch?"

Then, "Well, let's go". The weather was beautiful, the terrace of the Sip Babylone was there, two steps away, welcoming. The conversation, or rather, the quasi-monologue resumed, unrolled, expanded, undulated, unfolded, uncoiled... At five in the afternoon, the young journalist left Tallon, drunk with words, struck with amazement by the strange feeling of being more intelligent, of having landed on the shore of another world[1].

And, without realizing at the time, that Roger Tallon, with no reason whatsoever, just offered him six hours of his life, generously, pedagogically, gratuitously in all the meanings of the word.

It's just like Tallon to be into that behaviour, into that situation of exchange, speech, opening, sharing and availability.

"I think that all relationships are based on a misunderstanding," Tallon confirmed most seriously. The four hundred or so people—students, collaborators—whom he has formed and among whom one finds temperaments as diverse as Guy Boucher, Claude Braunstein, Alain Carré, Raymond Guidot, Marc Sadler... have listened well and retained the lesson perfectly.

Montaigne wrote: "To teach a child is not to fill a vase, but to light a fire." Tallon is not a hoarder of treasure, but a pyromaniac.

---

[1] One would have guessed that the young journalist in question is none other than the author of this text.

The pyromaniac obviously knew everything about the fire paintings of Yves Klein. As Yves Klein knew about the existence of Roger Tallon. In 1960, Paris was a village stirred by economic renewal and the rise of the consumer society. A consumer that people like Tallon and the New Realists would fundamentally question in extraordinarily different ways. For multiple reasons and several objectives.

Klein and Tallon were going to work together on an odd project which would take the designer back to his childhood memories, to Méliès and Mermoz combined, the Rocket Pneumatique, a sort of interplanetary bus. Tallon knew very well that Klein's dream was doomed to disintegration out of the earth's atmosphere, but he shared the vision both prophetic and poetic of the world that the artist expressed.

Pierre Restany remembered the young Tallon: "For me he embodied the breath of a visionary energy in everyday life."

Visionary. It is by being a visionary that Tallon became an artist. Even if he refused its practise, even if he decided to "stick" to everyday life. However, that will of the sign, information and communication, rather than of the object, corresponded to the essence of artistic creation itself. To appeal first to the look. To modify the look one directs onto the world in order to be able to change the world. "Art doesn't produce the visible, it makes visible," said Paul Klee.

At the very beginning was Ipoustéguy. Then came Klein and Adzak, César and Arman. Considered by the artists as a kind of "technical adviser", as a top-notch perfecter, Tallon was quickly

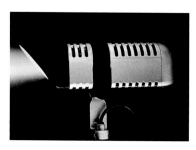

Spotlight for ERCO, 1973
Roger Tallon and *Veronic*, the 8 mm camera designed for Sem, 1957
Spotlight for ERCO, 1973

Téléavia TV set, 1969

changed into a partner. From that long parallel journey with the art world, Tallon has maintained his collaboration with *Art Press*, the magazine created, directed and animated by his friend Catherine Millet, whose graphic pattern he created in 1973, and for which he continues, month after month, designing the cover.

In 1970 Tallon was, and rightfully, charged with the planning of the French pavilion at the Exposition Universelle at Osaka in Japan. He went there to express as best he could his technological versatility, his imagination and his humour; calling on other designers and artists to make "the game more interesting," he said. Tallon shares, we know that. Through generosity, for sure, but also because he adores confrontation, indeed even opposition.

In parallel to the French pavilion, Tallon harbored another big project. He knew to what extent his friend Yves Klein, experienced judoka, had been influenced by Japan. He also knew that at the time, Klein was one of the only French people to have a certain notoriety in Japan. During lunch with the cultural attaché at the French Embassy in Tokyo, he suggested the organization of a big exhibition by the artist. "Marvellous idea," the cultural attaché replied. "I will be in Paris next month, can you organize a meeting with Mr Klein?" That scene happened in 1969 and Yves Klein died in 1962! Thirty years later, Tallon still fluctuates between anger, laughter and consternation. And remembers that, again in the 60s, the cultural attaché at the American Embassy had suggested to the director of the Ecole Nationale Supérieure des Beaux Arts (where architecture was still taught) to invite within his walls a big exhibition devoted to Mies van der Rohe. And the reply: "I have nothing against it, but first, I would like to see what that young miss is done..." Tallon's laughter, in those cases, is like his speech, torrential.

In the margins of art, but sometimes also an artist. Not acclaimed since he always signed his rare appearances with a pseudonym and doesn't like to dwell on those digressions which, apparently, belong to his secret garden. At best we know that he actively took part in the works of the group *Automat*, that he was engaged in strange projections with Roy Adzak in the house of André Bloc in Meudon, and that he practised what is today called video art well before its time. Because frontiers are rarely impervious, because Tallon is an assiduous experimenter, he has often been assimilated with the avant-gardes of the 20th century: De Stijl, Bauhaus, Constructionism, the New Spirit and, of course, Futurism. Some have even seen similarities between the Gallic Tower and Mondrian, between his luminous experimentations and Moholy-Nagy, between his cosmic dreams and Tatlin. In reality, Tallon doesn't recognize himself in any avant-garde, too busy is he to make the world tilt over in effective modernity.

And because Talon is a free spirit, one knows his reticence facing any adherence to a movement, a school, a clique... Tallon is much closer to Dada than to Surrealism, much more subversive than revolutionary, more like Picabia than Duchamp.

Rather than elaborate a dogma, rather than imagining the replacement of one order with another, rather than being interested in objects, even the *ready-made*, Tallon has always preferred to let his imagination run, to give total freedom to "amorous disorder" and to take interest in subjects rather than in objects. Tallon the designer obviously takes interest in bicycle wheels and bottle racks but Tallon the artist prefers to mould bottoms. Beautiful ones, preferably.

Talking about design, Tallon says: "Play, humour, fantasy, and eroticism are not forbidden to it."

In 1981, Milan exploded under the breaking Memphis wave. Led by Sottsass, all the Cibic, De Lucchi, Kuramata, Shire, Thun, Zanini... enjoyed themselves fully and practised joyfully play, humour, fantasy and eroticism. In reality their work practice was limited to the household world and they rarely landed on the shores of industry. It's the moment Tallon chose to declare in *Modo* magazine: "...Pesce, however, is not an artist; the artist is the one who masturbates; the designer, by contrast, makes love and his partner is industry. And as in France industries are rather frigid, you can imagine the result."

Tallon is undoubtedly fighting on all fronts, including the least expected.

And the one devoted to the "public transport" can be read in different ways. For there was something afoot in trains, métros, and funiculaires. From *North by Northwest* to *La Madone des Sleepings* and passing by "let's have a cuddler here and now," the examples are numerous and suggestive of infinite possibilities offered... To convince oneself, one just has to consider the comfort and discretion offered by the lower floor of the TGV Duplex and which sometimes changes into the Blue Train or the Bangkok-Chiang Mai.

Odd journeys devised by Tallon for a night club in Saint-Germain-des-Prés with the producer Raoul Lévy and for another

The Aspen conferences (from left to right): François Barré, Jean Baudrillard (from the back), Henri Ciriani and Roger Tallon
The dog Quitus and its splint

"day club" with the fated name, L'*Astrolabe*, have unfortunately never seen the light of day. Of it remains however the series "Module 400" whose main characteristic was a strange alveolar foam, called *spazmolla* and which covers chairs, stools and beds.

In 1966, Jacques Lacloche organized in his gallery an exhibition entitled "L'Objet 2". The metaphoric trapezoidal bed of the series was there. Above the bed, stuck on the wall, two underwater-diving tubes capped by a round red bulb, have been transformed into bedlights. The sleeping partner of the exhibition saw red as she looked at them: "How awful, they look like dicks!" And she had them pulled off immediately. Far from any fetishism, Tallon still has them at home, uses them and sees them as lights.

Duty of memory then. But a practical memory, put into work, generator of memories to come. Duty of friendship too. A faithful and active friendship.

At the end of the 60s, proximity compelled, Tallon was very Arnys, the famous men's shop at the Carrefour Sèvres-Babylone. Suit, tie, accessories, the real Parisian chic. One day, his nephews drag him to 41 rue du Temple, where he discovered a strange tailor who is passionate about materials, technique, comfort and the sign. Intrigued, Tallon buys a jacket. The day after he is back and renews his wardrobe completely. A meeting has taken place, a friendship born and Tallon has never ceased being dressed by Michel Schreiber. Moreover, as a convinced Schreiberophile, he draws along to the rue du Temple, then the rue de Birague his friends, collaborators and students. Even better, many suspect him of having co-founded "ADSA-partners" in 1984, not so much for creating a dream trilogy re-uniting Paulin, Schreiber and Tallon, than for making once and for all Michel and Roger live together.

In 1973, Nicole and Roger inherit a puppy, a short-haired dachshund which they decide, the year of the Q obliges, to call Quitus. Eight years later, following an accident, Quitus, his back broken, has his hind quarters completely paralyzed. Tallon set to work immediately. He wrote a notebook of specifications, set his team of Design Programmes SA that he had founded, in action. The research was hard, and the result uncertain. The meeting with a mechanic of the SNECMA would be needed for that project to finally succeed: a kind of all terrain cart mounted on wheels, which would leave speechless his worldwide colleagues, from Misha Black to Arthur J. Pulos, Josine des Cressonnières, and Tomas Maldonado. An exemplary success, equal to the splint invented by Charles Eames in the middle of the Second World War for the wounded American soldiers, and chosen as object of the century by Pierre Staudenmayer; Charles Eames is one of the rare designers often quoted by Roger Tallon.

Necessity is generator of invention, that's obvious. The cart and the splint demonstrate it abundantly.

But chance sometimes instigates curious meetings, odd associations. The name Tallon is of Irish and immemorial origin: one won't learn anything more. If not that word, *tallon*, means in English the back claw of the eagle. How not to see a sign there? From the eagle, Tallon has the Olympian sight, the eye in facets, a way of maintaining a general view of the world, of dominating the landscape quietly, then suddenly swooping down on his prey. Once again, the loop is looped.

Memory, friendship, fidelity, positivism, ambiguity, paradox, complexity, humour, rigor, pleasure, sharing, violence, compulsion, ingenuousness, curiosity, are all words that qualify to perfection Roger Tallon and which show what the man and the professional are capable of.

If one was not attentive, one would believe that they were only missing tenderness and nostalgia.

In the middle of the 80s, Tallon is having lunch on the terrace of the Tour d'Argent in the place de la Bastille with an associate and two clients. Tallon's eyes wanders around and stops at the corner of the rue de Charenton, on a demolition site in full swing, The Opéra Bastille operation has begun and Tallon was born there, at the very end of the rue de Charenton. His table companions reproach him for being inattentive. Tallon replied: "My past is being destroyed!" What he doesn't say is that the demolition is being carried out with a mechanical shovel he had drawn a few years before… again the loop is looped.

Sketching the portrait of Roger Tallon, is sketching the man, the creator and the professional in one single person. Flesh, thought and craft for all of them are with him definitely indissociable. Of that perilous game, it is undoubtedly his friend, the historian and art critic Catherine Millet, who make the most:

"...The one who is perhaps not so much a "barbarian"—a human being without culture devastating a civilized country—than an explorer—a civilized being who tests his knowledge on a wild country."

Roger Tallon as a soldier, around 1950
Roger Tallon on the *Taon* (horsefly), 1956

Imagination Powered

*I dedicate this interview to
Françoise Jollant Kneebone and Claude Braunstein,
with thanks to
Pierre Staudenmeyer and Frédéric Danos.*

Roger Tallon launched his career as a designer in the postwar context, when a handful of designers such as Jacques Viénot, Georges Patrix, and Henri Sargueil had begun speaking of an industrial aesthetic. At the time, France was undertaking its reconstruction on the basis of industrial planning, with the creation of powerful economic groups and the consequent decline of the small workshops unable to assimilate the new production models. Industrial design began to be practiced in the early fifties, following the path blazed by Tallon himself, the initiator of a style of "technological design" that would ultimately become predominant.

The man who is now known as "Mr. TGV" for his work on the French high-speed trains—a reductive label in view of the number and variety of projects he has carried out—offers us a chance to review almost a half-century of design practice, which he consistently theorized and envisaged in its totality. For Roger

Tallon always situates himself in the project, relying on an insatiable thirst for information of all kinds and in all forms, from the most apparently insignificant details to the fundamentals... His strength lies in his capacity to inventory, classify, and manage this sum of knowledge so as to render it fully active in his practice. The "Tallon system"[1] thus represents the operational mode of a curious man who became a designer by accident, as he likes to recall.

My interview with Roger Tallon was carried out from February 26 to March 15, 1999. At first I imagined that the text would take the form of a portrait from various angles, punctuated by the classic system of question-response. But Roger Tallon being an atypical man, I decided to construct this interview in his image, the better to convey the systematic, analytic, and analogical spirit that characterizes him. So this will be "an attempt at exhaustivity," somewhat like Georges Perec's observational descriptions of the thousand-and-one scenes of life unfolding on Saint-Sulpice square over a period of several hours.

I based myself on a number of broad themes, able to embrace the itinerary of a man with a free and progressive vision. In the face of the constant back-and-forth movement of Roger Tallon's memory, these different sections allow chronological order to take its place naturally: the last fifty years come into view through a long, wandering stroll through the heart of that half-century, as Roger Tallon engages in sudden swerves, turnabouts, and other digressions, via the free associations that he so enjoys.

The guiding thread of this text then becomes the designer's freedom to tell his own story. Memory unfolds.

[1] F. Jollant Kneebone, "Objets systèmes/systèmes d'objets," in *Roger Tallon, Itinéraires d'un designer industriel* (Centre Georges Pompidou).

Agence Design Programmes SA, 1973
Helicoïd stairs, aluminium, Lacloche gallery, 1966

Roger Tallon: I'm a bit lazy about opening the drawers of my memory. I have to explain to younger people that at a moment in life one no longer seeks to pile up too many memories; yet still our memory can't be saturated, and each day we continue to stock up, despite everything. It's a monster which is constructed little by little, like a pyramid. Which doesn't mean we tend to forget, but that it takes time to find things. Like searching around in the telephone book.

So did you plug in the machine? We're going to go way back...

Chloé Braunstein: It's rolling.

Roger Tallon: Right now! Whatever I feel like doing, I just do (says the song).

Habitat wants to reissue my "Zombies"[2] at the end of this year. I'm going to redesign them all: the dimensions will change, there's no reason why I should do the same thing twice. It's like if I were to redo my Téléavia: you can be sure it wouldn't be the same! Tom Dixon has chosen other things from my production, like my desk accessories, but he found my staircase "too Hollywood"![3] Just because he knows Jane Fonda has one.

I've got projects in every field. In transportation there are lots of things that haven't been produced and that I'm still attached too (in architecture as well). On the other hand, I've just come out with a line of glasses for the crystal maker Arnolfo de Cambio, under the art direction of François Burckhardt. The exercise

[2] *Zombies*: chairs designed for the Astrolabe café (Paris, Saint-Germain-des-Prés) in 1967.
[3] Spiral staircase in polished aluminum, produced by Lacloche (1964).

consists in asking people like Sottsass or Mari to do a project like the ones you do at school. Why not? Out of around twenty that I proposed, three were chosen. All of which makes me think I wouldn't have had a great career in the culinary arts... it's too much. I know a Finnish woman who has designed 300 place settings: for me, that's 299 too many! Once I had designed table settings myself, I decided I would never do any others and I've kept my word. So let the collectors be forewarned. For Christofle I created a transitional object for the third millennium, into which I've compacted history since J.C., a difficult synthesis... You have to work your way through, like sifting gravel, in order to extract the irreducible from the secondary. It's a 100% symbolic project.

I continually take notes and arrange my ideas in columns, in order to catalogue them properly. I don't bring the notebooks out very often, but they're useful from time to time. I cut out images, I make montages, collages, enlargements. My criteria is impact, and if it doesn't mean anything today it may tomorrow. There are things that come out of contemporary art, other things from illustration or advertising. Sometime soon I'm planning to take up activities of personal expression again, which I cut short in the seventies.

Contexts

I was fifteen in 1945: I'm from the generation immediately after the one that lost the war, I'm among those who didn't get all broken up. Around me people were being taken prisoner or deported, like my uncle to Mauthausen. My father and his friends, who were full of life in '39, came back demolished... At the time of the exodus, I was eleven and I saw my first dead man in a column of refugees (it was in Tours). We were moving slowly forward in my grandfather's beautiful Citroën and after an air attack I saw a guy lying on a pile of stones. I was thinking to myself it's no place for a siesta, when we came up close and I realized he was covered in blood... During the occupation I left Paris for lack of food. I was sent to my uncle's in the middle of the Resistance in the southeast, and mixed up in the rivalries between Gaullists and communists. On July 14, 1993, they almost came to blows, at the end of a dinner with one half singing the International and the other half, the Marseillaise. Later I was transferred to my god-father's, a dyed-in-the-wool Pétainiste who had bought an abbey and filled it with charcoal for his own trucks, but the resistance fighters in the region came to supply themselves by force. I took care of managing the stock, happy and proud to be useful.

In my universe as a child living through the war, what I felt was a "hyperactivist" situation, with the idea that everything happened to drum rolls and you had to take on project after project. My project was to become an aviator. And my model was Mermoz. I've always been a hybrid, an independent who never did what he was told. So the only academic degree I ever got came from England,[4] where I felt like an English vintner coming to Beaune to be get his wine-taster's credentials. I was on a

[4] RDI: Royal Designer for Industry, honorific degree awarded to Roger Tallon in Great Britain by the Royal Society of Arts (1973).

government grant. My father was an invalid, my parents didn't have the money and it wasn't easy... The whole school period was a burden. So I'll sum it up quickly.

First there's my mother, a former head seamstress with Patou who had become a teacher. She was avid for culture and had participated in the foundation of Jeunesses Musicales, a musical program for French youth. My sister and I were part of her quota, every week she brought us either to the opera or to chamber-music concerts which finally bored me (overdose!) and made me prefer the cinema.

My mother wanted me to become an artist because I used to draw a lot, but I wouldn't have stood being in art school: what kind of sense does that make, going to school to be an artist? César once told me, "Art school isn't a real school. I never learned anything there, but it's great for making friends!" At that time old César was down and out, the art school was his hotel. I always sketched everything, over and over again. I did caricatures, humorous drawings, comic books... I loved American comics and super-heroes like Flash Gordon. I took all that very seriously.

The cinema was my real school: at a certain point I went three times a day. I was even a member of the Ciné-club at the Musée de l'Homme. For me, cinema was American above all. They go together. I became conscious of democracy with American cinema, because I never had the impression that France was a democracy, even if we'd had the Popular Front. We had lived under Pétain, and we'd had the extreme right before and during the war.

In 1948 I found myself as part of the occupation in Germany with the Americans, in a destroyed country that was rebuilding

Series *Module 400*
- trapezial metamorphic bed, the "Objet 2" exhibition, Lacloche gallery, Paris 1966
- stool and (survel) low-backed-chair, Lacloche ed., 1965

itself thanks to the German women. We were dressed like Americans, the cigarettes were American, the tanks and the rations were American! I Americanized myself. For me, there wasn't any other way. And maybe that's the heart of the story: living in a society where I imagined there would be no distinction of origins (even if it isn't that way in reality). At the time I felt that we had definitively become "Gallo-rican." At the same time, why go to America, the homeland of design, whereas here in France there was so much adventure in virgin territory? As foreseen, I studied for the Air School entry exam, a dry kind of world where I stood out because I sketched, was involved in theater and journals… The Picasso of the class! "Atypical, but a good student." Everything that I still find useful today came from those fundamental studies, to which I owe the fact that I've never had technical problems with my clients and have been able to communicate well with the technicians.

The army was also a great place to learn communication skills, since in 1947 I was in the "military information" service in Germany; it was the beginning of the Cold War.

Styles(s)

At our house it was more or less the "Cosy Corner" style: I hated that because it was cheap. As a general rule, everything I saw was dull and ugly. I was merciless! Finally I even found the people ugly. I didn't have any ideas about architecture, but I despised everything that was old and dirty…

If I had to locate my take-off point in terms of form in general, I think it took place in 1937 thanks to the World Exhibition of Arts and Technologies in Modern Life. Suddenly in this ugly universe there was a breath of fresh air. I discovered the Corbusier pavilion, the Spanish pavilion and many others, in a universe that was refreshing even if it was fake, where everything seemed possible: and if you could do that, you could change all the rest. Everything fascinated me, and above all the details. That way of looking at things never left me and later, when I worked on major exhibitions, I used to say to myself: if this can manage to trigger off such passions in children, it's worth doing.

You can't get away from the question of style. Proof: there's a poster reserved for customs agents dealing with furniture, which begins with King Dagobert and ends with Pompidou, referenced as "design style." A style is linked together by features that allow you to identify it. In my work I'm not concerned with that, because I've above all designed machines. When I began, the people doing technical design had very little involvement with habitat, or simply through kitchen appliances. Just episodic excursions.

The preoccupation with style always comes back at the heart of the polemics on design, it's also the major concern of certain deco-designers who put a strong imprint on their objects. That's a resolutely artistic attitude. I think the work of the responsible designer is to operate in such a way that the objects are charged with the least possible pressures and suprematist values: humble, discreet, and durable, with the least imposition of emotion; otherwise they become invasive and unbearable. That was the idea behind the work of someone like Nizzoli,[5] for example: restful, tranquil objects…

To speak of style when it's a matter of design is to admit a misunderstanding from the very start. Compared to what we were looking for in the great period of the Ulm School[6] and functionalism, design has gone off track today. It's a race for differential marketing, like contemporary artistic creation which is sliding off toward the dominant market. It's the same thing for design. I think that at a given moment, the objects conform to fashion. So people remind us that in the sixties there were lots of bright colors… Sure, but the real reason is that plastic appeared and it finally made the bright colors possible. Before, if you wanted to make furniture orange or green you had to paint it. With plastic you could do whatever you liked. For me, style/fashion and design remain irrevocably contradictory.

Design

I the early fifties I temporarily took a job in the research office of an electromechanics company, and so I began putting together products without knowing I was doing design. It was gratifying and well paid. So I could have become an electrical engineer while

[5] Marcello Nizzoli, Italian designer, creator of the first Olivetti machines (1887-1969).
[6] Ulm School (Hochschule für Gestaltung), German school founded in 1953, closed in 1968. Max Bill gave the dimension of a design school to what was initially a political and literary project. Ulm was based on a highly elaborated technical, economic, and cultural knowledge of the processes of fabrication, distribution, and consumption. It invented the functional object which was supposed to emancipate the individual and refute the traditional means of seduction that render the user dependent on misleading illusions, thus avoiding enslavement to consumption (cf. *Dictionnaire international des arts appliqués et du design*, Editions du Regard, 1996).

continuing to draw comics. Design really began for me when I was contacted by an American company of public contracting material, Caterpillar, who were looking for someone to coordinate their technical and commercial communication. I began working for them and learned photo-engraving and publishing, in particular. When I created the catalogues I had to use American techniques: for Caterpillar the important thing was not the graphics, the important thing was to do it in a professional way.

In 1953, a former classmate who was working in the patent department at Dupont de Nemours asked me to come over and talk with them: they were looking for a designer. That's where I heard the word "design" for the first time. They explained to me that it was "someone who does what you did at school: drawing automobiles, planes, and so on." So for two years I sketched lots of machines for Dupont de Nemours, working freelance. For example, I had to draw in white pencil against a black ground, American style, with little "flashes": "Are you capable of doing that?" That's where I worked with the inventor of cellophane film, Brendenberger, who drilled into me the purely scientific and philosophical notion of the continuous: any break in the load brings about disorder and loss. So everything had to be continuous, production had to be continuous, sales continuous... The idea of just-in-time. The same year, our photographer informed me that a lecture was taking place at the Compagnie Française de l'Édition: "The Beauties of Technology."[7] It was the beginnings of the industrial aesthetic, and Jacques Viénot[8] told about what was

[7] "Les Beautés de la technique," lecture given in 1953 by Jacques Viénot at the Compagnie Française d'Édition (Paris).

happening in America. I went to see him at the end of the talk and explained that I was very interested by his ideas, because I was already practicing that activity. I wasn't the only one: we were a spontaneous generation discovering, amidst a total desert, that this strange thing—design—actually existed. He had been a decorator and situated himself in the modern art movement. At the time, Jacques Viénot directed Technès, but except for Parthenay[9] he was very much alone. We went to have a drink and I saw Fernand Léger come up to shake his hand, and Cocteau a little while later... I was very impressed. He subsequently hired me and I remained with Technès until 1973: I had my freedom, I educated myself and signed my products.

Learning

Though I had read a great deal, I had never taken up the problems of architecture or the modern movements. It was foreign to me. I suddenly came to them through Viénot who directed his own journal and knew prominent people from around the world. Through Viénot I discovered the Milan Triennial and Italian design. A fantastic opportunity: I was able to meet Ponti, Le Corbusier, Nizzoli... It was a total and immediate widening of my horizons.

[8] Jacques Viénot, French industrialist and theorist (1893-1959), author in 1940 of *La République des arts*. In 1949 he founded Technès, a bureau of technical and aesthetic design studies. In 1951 he founded the Institut d'Esthétique Industrielle, which from 1953 onward would publish the journal Design Industriel. He was also the inventor of "Label France," later destined to become "Beauté Industrie." With Sir Paul Reilly, he was one of the cofounders of the ICSID (International Council of Societies of Industrial Design) created in Paris on June 28, 1957.

[9] Jean Parthenay, French industrial designer born in 1919. He worked for Technès from 1948 to 1978.

I'd heard of Loewy at the time when his book was published in French.[10] I almost even worked with him, but it was something like an ad agency which as many sales reps as designers. I didn't like that. Loewy wasn't a liar but he avoided telling the truth; because he didn't draw himself… At that time there were some really big names in the United States, like Henry Dreyfuss,[11] Walter Dorwin Teague,[12] and many others… I was mainly interested in the designers who did appliances and machines, rather than furniture.

Viénot organized a course in Paris[13] and I began teaching there: an entire generation of designers came together with very little difference in age between us. When I set up the Industrial Design section at the Decorative Arts school,[14] I explained to the students that I was at the same point as them: I didn't know anything more, but I had a lot of practical experience. Today I'd say that design education has exploded and is heading toward fractalized approaches that are much less exciting than in my time.

Theorizing Practice

With all this intensive practice there was no time for theory. Information came from all over the world and showed us what was going on. Even today I still wonder how we could do all that at once, with more than fifty studies a year, sometimes seven in the

[10] La Laideur se vend mal, Raymond Loewy, 1953 for the French translation.
[11] Henry Dreyfuss, American designer (1904-1972). He is also the author of *Designing for People* (1955).
[12] Walter Dorwin Teague Sr., American industrial designer (1883-1960).
[13] Advanced course in industrial design, founded in1956 at the École Supérieure des Arts Appliqués.
[14] ENSAD: École Nationale Supérieure des Arts Décoratifs.

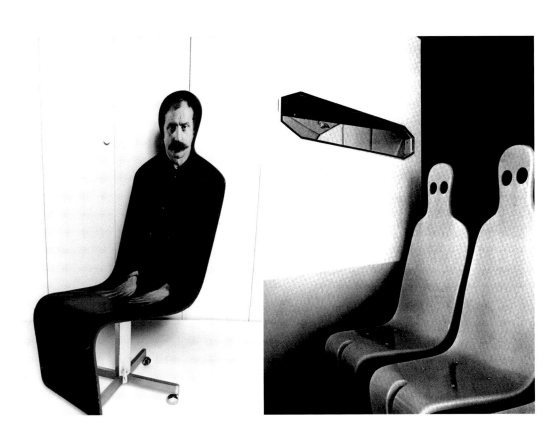

Portraits-seats series, here César, 1967
Zombies seats for the *Astrolabe* café in Paris, 1967

course of a single month. Terrifying! I also worked with Viénot on the promotion of exhibitions. At the time there were very active movements like Formes Utiles (Useful Forms).[15] I functioned theoretically by autopsying real projects, and I quickly chose my "camp," that of "ultra-strict" functionality. I saved time by theorizing things while they were being made.

The Designer

The designer is not the White Knight. His role is prescribed within industrial production, he stands out by his ability to transform a set of conflicting constraints into a legible, useful product, adding value and often innovating. This means that the designer, no less than other contributors (technicians, sales people) must invent new realities.

That's where I differ from Ettore Sottsass who says that the designer is only a shaper. I'm convinced that the best shaper is one who is also capable of inventing.

Reduced to its most simple expression, the definition of the designer's trade is: "someone who makes things and lives off that activity." He does studies and develops them, therefore he is! In the sixties I would bring my class of students over to the Useful Forms exhibition; I observed them and I could immediately make out who was predisposed and who wasn't. The ones who were "in" were very positive, looked closely at things, tried to understand without drawing attention to themselves. There were

---

[15] Formes Utiles, association founded in 1949 for the inaugural exhibition of the UAM (Salon des Arts Ménagers).

also those who were detached from everything, the "outs" who were interested in nothing. And finally the "in-and-outs," the one who criticized everything superficially, with stereotypical ideas. A designer conceives things realistically and consciously. Maybe the definition is a bit rudimentary, but that limits the field. Afterwards, talent is something else.

Design Today

I'd say one never attains a level of pure design. Today I'm trying to get as close as possible. What I call militant design was an "event" with which I was closely associated. In those days we used to talk a lot, not ontologically, but in a concrete, formative way. We were doing contemporary design in action, and we watched what the others did without any jealousy. On the contrary, we said: "How could it be done better?" I was part of that energy and for me it was positive. Design today doesn't have adventure any more, it's a polemic, like art and architecture today are polemics. We even see the return of manners that seemed guaranteed never to reappear. Architecture, for its part, has been amazingly transformed into a headstrong competition for virtuosity.

In the word design, there was always the word "good," which meant providing a good response to the problem. The history of this "Good Design" covers several different periods. The one we belonged to is quite recent, and Charles Eames could characterize it quite well: a certain Anglo-Saxon humanism, which meant that American industry, with all the wealth it brought, raised this practice to its apogee. For their part, the Italians emerging from fascism found their clients in a tissue of enlightened project commissioners and businessmen, who worked with creators as they did in the Renaissance (Olivetti, for instance).

Is design in a process of dissolution today? Elie Faure has written a history mixing all the arts—the history of the arts through human beings. There I discovered the theory of the true "imaginary museum," where art history comes down to a succession of oscillations. Take Romanesque art for instance: integrated into love, by which I mean passion, the believers; rough and clumsy forms, but very expressive. Then you go up and up and it's the apogee: for example, the century of Pericles. Everything radiates. It's part of a rich economic cycle where masterworks are born. Then, dissolution in criticism: back down again. You get the effects, the drapery, the mannerism. So modern design could be summed up as a short-lived adventure, linked to the three phases of the industrial revolution: integration to the passion, fulfillment amidst abundance, dissolution in criticism.

Object vs. Product

Our trade consists in transforming ideas into objects, then into products. A corkscrew made with a twisted nail is an artisanally fabricated object. A product is a molded corkscrew, fabricated in quantity, and integrated to the system that makes it functional: packaging, instructions for use, sales techniques. So the product is a mutation, what's left of the object when it enters general use. The designer will fabricate millions of corkscrews which will be impossible to straighten after their industrialization. It's in this sense that the designer is responsible: he can't make a mistake and tends necessarily toward perfection.

My incursions into things involving the intimate sphere, the "sanctuary of the home," happened via collective facilities. Mainsi, my staircase, came into existence because I was a consultant for the foundrymen's union.[16] I proposed an exhibition at the CNIT[17] where I wanted to show that cast iron could be presented in a different way and that it wasn't necessarily limited to radiators and machine tools. Via furniture I could start dealing with technical and artistic cast iron. At the time there were no contemporary staircases in cast iron. So mine became a trendsetter.

The president of the goldsmiths' union wanted me to make models of knives and forks:[18] "It doesn't interest me to just draw knives and forks," I said, "but a full table setting, yes!" Because I have a systematic mind, I realized I couldn't sell this setting: in the marketing system of the time it wasn't possible to distribute a complete table setting, because the people distributing the plates didn't distribute the knives and forks. A real brain twister! So I decided that my table settings would leave the national network, for a foreign network distributing Scandinavian design. So that's how I sold these French-made table settings as import products! And to simplify the sale, I established codes to give ideas of sets: knives and forks for summer, for winter…

[16] CIFOM: Syndicat Professionnel des Fondeurs.
[17] Batimat 1964, at the CNIT.
[18] Système 3T (1967): table settings, produced by Ravinet d'Enfert; dishware, produced by Raynaud; glassware, produced by Daum.

Graphic Design

Everything is graphic at first. For example, it's no use studying an object if it doesn't have visual meaning and semiological characteristics. It's a way of "looping the communications loop" with very few elements. Because graphic design isn't limited to beautiful letters and nice colors. It can't be an end in itself.

I've always thought that a professional designer was someone complete, with preliminary training in 2-D, able to master flat surfaces before moving on to volume: the good students were those who "moved through the layers." Not only did I direct some of them towards a specialization in graphics, but I also ensured that industrial and graphic design would go side by side at the ENSAD. As far as the teaching of graphics goes, I always referred to the Zurich school: the Swiss have excellent technical and methodological training, and the French have a little too much imagination, to the detriment of precision. The day when you can combine the two, it's a happy couple.

The Collection

I'm afraid of accumulation, even though I'm an obsessional like most designers, like Achille Castiglione with his bric-a-brac objects. Since I have an open way of working, I bounce off objects and ideas. But I don't think a collection can be like a data bank, at best it's a "life bank," an "experience bank," with the underlying idea of making it fruitful, cross-fertilizing the stocks. So the collection becomes something like finance.

Classic Plastics

Of course the materials are decisive. For example, I don't use plastic if the product was initially conceived to be in aluminum. In the fifties there was almost no plastic: it was a cheap kind of material for inexpensive products. People just knew it as "plastic." Now one speaks of plastics in the plural, in order to be precise: carbons, composites, etc. For me, it's an intelligent way of getting further into the material… I'd say that today the important thing is not what plastic did for me, but rather what I did for it, how I stressed its qualities.

Nonetheless, I'm nostalgic for certain injected metals: they had weight, and the things they were used for had a lot of personality, like cameras.

Systoms

When I begin working on a project, my first reflex is to analyze all the data, a method that lays out all the aspects of the problem at hand, including the ones that don't seem to have any relation with the subject. Then comes the study of the quantitative, qualitative, economic, psychological, and social aspects… In short, everything that can enrich my knowledge of the subject. Then comes the attempt at synthesis, through hypotheses which consist in finding out whether it works. Let's take an example: the glass. We didn't always drink from glasses. The appearance of an object for drinking comes from hollow horns, without a base. We knew nothing about Pasteur, so we all drank successively from the same container. There was also the bowl… Little by little, we oriented

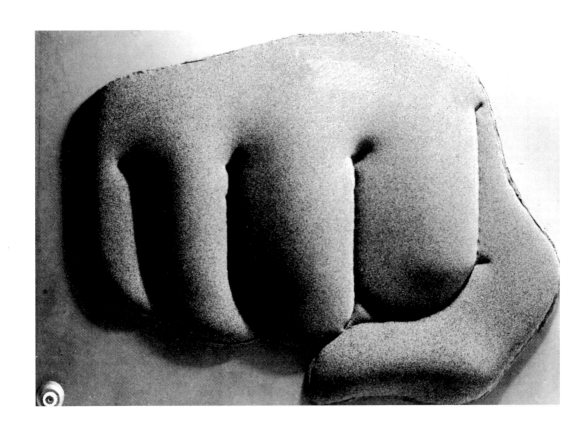

Le Poing (The First), " La Main" (The Hand) exhibition, Claude Bernard gallery,
Paris, 1965

Automat, research on the three dimensional projections, reception form of the projection, 1970

ourselves toward a definite container, but still a community one, until the bourgeois period when you had to have everything individually: glasses, forks, knives... So let's continue with the possibilities: drinking with a straw, or returning to the bottle, which had long served as a direct distributor. Let's also take an extreme situation, that of the astronaut, for whom it is impossible to drink in from a glass: how to keep the liquid from coming out through the nose? He has to suck... The possibilities gives you a good way of thinking about whether there are reasons to change anything: it's such a pleasure to lift your elbow! The glass will remain just as long as people enjoy drinking. (Because why not imagine that one day man will no longer need to drink?)

You reach the possible when you are faced with the sum of all the items issuing from the existent. It's mathematical: figures will appear with percentages that indicate the positives and negatives. Then it's a matter of setting forth hypotheses to produce a new situation which should be better than the one before. An improvement. We relate the points in question to retain the maximum number of positive points, because if we lose as much as we gain, the entire game is not worth the effort. The idea is that with the changes, the balance sheet should be positive. That's the objective. You do that in a sensible way by setting forth a hypothesis, then a proposal, which you reject later on. You have to look for another one, keeping the most open mind possible: a designer should be capable of changing gears very quickly, because the more he lingers, the less likely is he to succeed—he just gets stuck.

So we have moved from the dissecting table to the lab where the "hypotheses" are made, and then confronted with experience.

That's what I did in the field of transportation, with the systematic use of tests. By carrying out this process of validation, you limit the number of proposals. Then you go into action with multi-criteria analysis, a kind of booby-trap which, when blindly applied, brings up very little. The difficulty of this analysis is to assign coefficients to the criteria: such an approach requires relatively strong coefficients, allowing you to zoom in and create a distortion which may be interesting.

In a project, the probable is rarely dealt with, except when you have to make a choice among possibilities: if probability consists in knowing the direction to take, then within the possibilities you might as well choose what's headed that way. The probable then becomes a kind of telescope for the making of a present-day choice, and it is employed in the research. We call that "discovery grids." For the watchmaker Lip that would consist, for example, in diagnosing what had been done and what could be done. Elaborating a discovery grid means constructing a system by introducing parameters, thanks to a *syntactic* code that touches on the mechanical and physical constitution of a product. *Pragmatics* is linked to its use and function. *Semantics* represents its symbolic value. On the syntactic level, an automobile is a metal box with wheels, a motor, a steering wheel, a turn signal... In this case, pragmatics consists in saying that a car is better than a horse: an object ready for use that moves when you decide and allows an individual to cover five hundred miles in a day, whereas on foot he can only do fifteen or twenty. There are other advantages: you can bring the baggage and the kids too! The semantic field is what this car represents in terms of image, its category and its price. It's the difference between a Volkswagen and a Rolls: a rich man may find it very important to possess a Volkswagen, and a Gypsy, a Rolls! So there are crisscrossed intentions. On that basis and by following those fields, we have covered three approaches which, when they are conjugated, serve to define a product pretty well.

Since I think of myself as an "orthodox" designer, I don't question the semiological code and I'm suspicious of pheno-menology. But I don't neglect structuralism! Because it's so much more exciting to work on signs and not on behaviors, which have more to do with anthropology…

Method

A big program has its demands, its conditions, and can't be carried out the same way as a small program. But what's gratifying for the designer? Some says it's hearing their name (the ego). The gratification can also come from money. But the money is inversely proportional to the continuity of success: if you fleece your clients, you're sunk! And I didn't choose design to become a millionaire… Do I have the satisfaction of finishing a job? No. I'd say that the real gratification is when you've solved a problem. It's the feeling of your own usefulness.

I think that designing a collection of glasses is no less gratifying than creating the TGV. For example, I designed a movie camera in '57, which today serves as a model for digital cameras.[19] But on the other hand, if I had only designed small objects I'd be frustrated—even if you get the most pleasure from the "little

---

[19] Movie camera *Véronic* 8 mm, for Sem (1957).7).

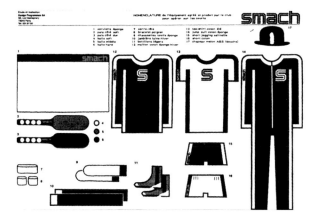

SMACH project, nomenclature of the equipment to operate on-courts, 1979
Polyurethane foam counter-project for the French Pavillon in Osaka, 1970

things," because you're really responsible for them. So you have to like changing scale.

I like to carry out big programs, because if you finish them reasonably well, then it's great. Even though they're not the source of the most satisfaction in terms of perfection, because there are too many parameters, too many accidents and interferences along the way. You often get to a more or less acceptable result in the end, but it's not the same pleasure as if you've made, for example, the "TS" folding chair, which is highly graphic and becomes three dimensional with a single gesture.[20]

When a program like the TGV begins, I commit myself for five years… In the beginning it's total freedom. There are constraints, but there's lots of room for action: you make proposals, there are exchanges, there are tests, then you start the game and you decide! That's when the program, strictly speaking, begins: a long underground period where you're going to spar with innumerable bits of program. The overall project is in your head and you have to be capable of reconstituting it at any moment. Sometimes by major groups, sometimes by little elements, hundreds of items. Certain pieces, even if they don't directly involve the design, have to go straightaway into production. So there are things which aren't important but are urgent; and others which are very important and only come at the end of the program. Sometimes I discover what I really did at the same time as my clients, or even as my users. Now and then an element arrives. It seems finished. But once set into place, you realize that it fits poorly. It's what I call a "duck." These

---

[20] "TS," model of folding chair, produced by Sentou (1978).

stages are like orchestration: the day when the composer puts together the brasses and the violins, he realize that what he has spent months on is not acceptable. So he corrects. But unlike him, the designer can't change anything: the industrial cycle has been kicked off and everything depends on his capacity to manage the situation, by limiting the number of ducks. When the designer begins his career, he makes a lot of ducks: he gets really disappointed and sometimes even gives up. But if he perseveres, their number diminishes: that's the reality of our trade when applied to major projects. If I design a wastebasket, I do a model first. And even if the molds aren't well made, I can do them over or touch them up without too much damage.

Mathematics

I've gained a rigorous way of reasoning from mathematics. It's not necessary to know math to do design, but the mathematical mind ought to interest everyone. The kind of rejection that consists in thinking that anything involving mathematics is inhuman, while everything human is gushy with emotion, is completely out of date… A good deal of mathematical reasoning is elegant and partakes of poetry. What I like is finding the solution thanks to mathematical elegance, attaining a penetrating result with an economy of means. And if the work is easy, if there's nothing painful and you haven't spent entire nights to extract the quintessence of the problem—then it's even more of a pleasure. But the teaching of math is such that people hate it, whereas it ought to be a distraction, but in concrete relation to what you have to deal with: working on signs to which values will be assigned later...

Theory and Movements

In our history of design there are far too many notions which have never been made explicit, and nobody worries about it. There is no specific criticism of this field, even though lots of intellectuals have dealt with the question... I'm thinking of Jean Baudrillard, for example, who left the field behind.

I'd say that France, a country with a rural tradition, is not really motivated by design, and the big bosses here are dirt farmers more than businessmen, without any particular taste for the industrial-cultural. Where I myself am concerned, I don't have a public position and I rarely take part in the fundamental debates in France: I think there really aren't that many, it's mostly just promotional! If I happen to meet a journalist and I tell him what I've got under my hat, it's taken as a polemic. The real debate on modernity doesn't interest anyone.

Modernism and Modernists

Among the current polemics, there's the one about postmodernism. They talk about postindustrial, but it's always got a whiff of postmodernism. Modernism is the ebb and flow of ideas. There was a grand, almost spellbinding period, when modernism was the great hope, then things went wrong and its application revealed the reality of some of its negative effects. Consequence:

disappointment or rejection. And yet the innovative powers are intact, the conflicts are reduced or have temporarily disappeared, because reason seems to have triumphed. Then we witness a return of the irrational which we attempt to rationalize. It becomes too sophisticated to produce any kind of credible commitment.

Myself, I remain a radical modernist since I don't believe there has been any failure of modernity, just that modernity has been carried out summarily, approximately. It remains despite everything the major path, because the ones being suggested today are just sidestreets; to move forward the creative spirit needs space and can't get lost in labyrinths or wander aimlessly in mirages...

If functionalism was thrown into doubt, that's because it was undeniably rudimentary—but you have to remember that we were just emerging from total primitivism! The demands of the modernist insurrection were rapidly satisfied, but with very basic solutions: so the failure is discernible, but not conclusive. I think we should continue in the same direction. On the other hand, criticism should deal with the quality of a functionalism that covers all the fields, including those linked to psychology, to lifestyles and acquired behaviors...

Functionalism hasn't really functioned: it hasn't gotten to the bottom of the problems, and its experiments haven't been conclusive. Though architecture isn't the only domain where this "thing" happened, it's definitely the one where the negative experiments show up the most clearly. It led to an excessive, violent city planning, reductive and destructive, onto which were superimposed phenomena of cultural mixtures which weren't properly taken into account. But I think functionalism was condemned too soon, and now we're wallowing around in a blur, with Byzantine debates. We have to go much further, much deeper, in the definition of the functional and of its fields, particularly by combining the functionalisms without treating them in a single, narrow way: a car is useful for getting around, but for lots of other things too! The idea would be a "transfunctionalism": the capacity to juggle with notions that bring forth other possibilities, ones that can justify the work to be done and the satisfactions to be gained from it. Change for the sheer sake of change is sterile (like art for art's sake).

Currently, modernism is considered out of style: postmodernism is supposed to be the only thing that makes sense. Myself, I find it pretty unhealthy to speak of postmodernism! In fact, Tomás Maldonado said that France was still somewhere in premodernism.[21] That's also what I'd say about the decorative arts movement: we haven't succeeded in getting rid of style. When we speak of modernism, it's above all in architecture and its various trends. In the fifties, there was a double revolution: the creative people were "neo-Art Deco," and that, apparently, already meant being modernist. I was in favor of that movement, even if I had a few reservations about Le Corbusier and his strict Calvinism. Its effects—like simplicity—encouraged me. In a lot of fields we're still in the nineteenth century, even if that's changing thanks to informatics. But from 1950 to 1970 you had to break down, and above all reconstruct, by putting out hypotheses. It's the whole

[21] 21. Tomàs Maldonado, professor and theorist of design born in 1922 in Buenos Aires. Invited by Max Bill in 1954, he taught until 1968 at the Ulm School, which he directed from 1964 to 1968.

3T line (china designed for Raynaud, stainless steel cutlery for Ravinet d'Enfer and cristal glasses for Daum), Sola France distribution, 1967

history of active thought. Today I miss that kind of enthusiasm, there are references to the images of the past, but the essentials interest people very little. They're so engrossed with style!

The fifties were the years of emergent postmodernism, which linked back to a historical continuity that finally consists in furnishing the rising new bourgeoisie... I had a breakaway position, because I worked with Jacques Viénot for whom design was only the continuity of the decorative arts. Maybe that's why he called design the "industrial aesthetic": but the fact of Frenchifying the practice got on my nerves, because design came from the Anglo-Saxons. Design as a discipline doesn't come out of our culture, but it has to become part of it and work as part of it. On the other hand, I was very respectful of what was happening in architecture, because there something was really happening. It has been denounced, but to my mind, this rejection of modernism in favor of postmodernism is suspect. Morally suspect: the recourse to the ancient, the return to egotism, to individuality. In a certain way you could speak of a return to a form of neofascist celebration, a sad successor to modernism... But I'm not convinced that modernism is really dead, because far too many references to it subsist within us.

Functionalism and the Decorative Arts

As there was no movement linked to design in the France of the fifties, the Decorative Arts school dictated the law. The exponents of Useful Forms were acid-tongued theorists who didn't practice design themselves... or only in limited domains. So the movement didn't take on any breadth. The conservatives who wanted to pass for enlightened patrons bought their production, but it didn't go any further. (Some of them bought Eames furniture[22] in the United States: there was a clientele, and that's when Knoll was born). The decorative arts people had gotten a smattering of modernism and they wanted to do the same thing to design, which represented a fundamental questioning of style. I had no affinity for the decorative arts, not being from a bourgeois background. But I figured that functionalism and the decorative arts could live in parallel, without harming each other…

Functionalism was in architecture like in everything else. The only thing that you can say now is that it was put down by people who couldn't make the long haul, who didn't understand the value of going down that road and persevering. Because the true functionalism is design. That's what assured the break with all we had done before. We try, before drawing anything at all, to understand all the parameters of the process, by selecting the functions to be fulfilled. We call that "functionalism" because we want it to function, which is the least you can expect. But functionalism is not an end in itself, it's a method of creation, even though it's quite easy to say whether a thing is functional or not: as soon as a chair doesn't fall down when you sit on it or a glass doesn't leak when you fill it with water, it's minimally functional…

There's also this eternal quarrel functionalism/need. Because the theory of needs doesn't exist, need is "unlimitable": first we need water, oxygen, and only then come the "needs/desires."

[22] 22. Charles and Ray Eames, two American designers. Charles Eames (1907-1978), Ray Eames (1912-1988).

Which means that once a certain number of basic functions have been fulfilled... Need is revealed above all by the perception of what the Other has. In short, functionalism has to go further than the simple, basic products, to reach the symbolic level. In the fifties, I discovered Claes Oldenburg who for me was doing a caricature of demiurgical American design. It wasn't so much a style as a manner. Oldenburg reproduced ordinary objects at a giant scale, which gave them a mythical dimension. In this way he made a plea for friendly objects. Until that point I had designed products with "tight, hard forms," and then I started doing more feminized objects, rounder, like the Corail, whose ambiance was born from that reaction. It was the great moment of rupture that combined with the reflection going on at the Ulm school, and which essentially entailed working on a new and clear basis, unburdened of any nostalgia.

The Ulm School

Ulm is the intellectual circle where I discovered Gestalt theory, as opposed to the associative psychology of the nineteenth century. Because of its political origins, since it was founded in memory of the German resistance fighters and martyrs, its pedagogical objective was to link back to the experimentation of the Bauhaus, interrupted by the Nazis. You have to understand that the Bauhaus was not a decorative arts school, but an attempt to promote a synthesis of art and technology, to meld together all the problems that had sprung up at a certain moment of humanity, and also to permit the beginnings of answers for the environment of the future. Since Ulm generated certain formal consequences, it was wrongly made into a style. I recently saw a Wagenfeld exhibition in his little museum in Bremen: he was a "pre-Ulmian," he didn't bother with style.

In the fifties, Ulm was the only place where something was happening in terms of design, and I continue to think that what happened there changed all the rest entirely. But its militant extremism caused the whole adventure to accelerate. After all, pedagogical experiments always end that way. If Ulm had continued, it would have probably culminated in a univocal formalism moving toward the non-object, toward a complete absence of visibility.

I have always done machines, whereas most of the designers were doing objects. So there was no contradiction in my work: a machine doesn't need anything symbolic, even if in the history of machinism—above all in the nineteenth century—there have been mechanisms charged with symbols, very close to ornamentation.

Today, when measured against "transfunctionalism," you can conclude that Ulm's functionalism didn't go beyond certain limits, rendering it a little too systematic. For example, there wasn't any psychic approach. After Ulm, some of the most advanced designers launched upon the semiological approach, structuralism in the more neutral sense giving way to the semiological instrument.

Although the best period of Ulm is the one when Hans Gugelot[23] began "revisiting" domestic equipment, my relation to that current of reflection really concretized through the critique of

[23] Hans Gugelot, Dutch designer (1920-1965). He taught at Ulm from 1956 to 1965.

Tomás Maldonado. I had been led to the terrain of a theory materialized by the inquiry into working methods, research, and the construction and elaboration of hypotheses: designing is the contrary of just finding, it entails seeking, then making choices to obtain the schema that's the richest in solutions.

At bottom, the idea was to understand what one found, to clarify its conception. You'll never reach the perfect conclusion in this field, but the least of things is knowing what you want and not letting yourself get carried away by your instincts. The big fashion today is to say that you have to know how to draw to do design. It's completely wrong: design doesn't need reflexivity, and the master's touch is a matter of know-how and not creativity!

Progress

Progress is not only knowing what's going to happen, but also what has happened. When a Formula 1 driver wins a race and stays ahead, it's not just because he drives well, but more because he keeps his curves together: in his head he's always two turns down the road.

So progress is a way of living. Everybody ought to be interested in progress. I accept the idea that some people are turned toward the past. Or toward nothing at all, why not! But hey, if you're not interested in what's coming next, it's a pretty sad state of affairs…

Being interested in progress is already a good approach. But being progressive means wanting things to go intrinsically better, and I think those interested in progress are motivated by exactly that. I'm very critical, so I'm not too "science-fiction" in the optimistic sense. Nor am I a pessimist, but I think that if those with good intentions are more numerous than those with bad ones, then it ought to improve existence in general.

Internet is a phenomenon that's completely unanalyzable on the basis of our old references: we don't have any benchmarks to grasp it by. In the means employed it's a matter of new technologies, based on a shrinkage of the planet's communication space. It's also a dazzling "leap" in terms of its effects: you can fit an encyclopedia into a little wafer! And it's going to bring some new developments in the question of languages: if you have speech recognition today, then by compensation there'll necessarily be recognition of idioms. And then simultaneous translation is also going to come out of that, like a new kind of language. I got to know Internet in '73 through "Technotec," a system conceived by some French programmers with Control Data: a terminal was installed at my home and I was able to use it. When you consulted you had to pay, when you were consulted you paid: a fluctuating account calculated in words per year. It only had to do with technological and computer-science problems. It was by using it that I became conscious that a revolution in communication was underway: it's like if I opened the window and called out "does anybody have a thing like that?" and the cry was heard from Tokyo to Timbuktu. I also saw another advantage: if I asked for something and there was no answer, that meant there was no one else currently active on that question. That too is information—negative information. Internet was an extension of the Technotec system, which was already too limited…

So that's how I arrived in the middle of the Minitel project in 1980. Today I'm working on the "next Minitel," direct, continuous, interactive spatial communication. You can't even imagine the consequences that this new system is going to have on our relational behaviors.

Utopias

Design has been way too dramatized, way too invested in the dream of transforming the world: utopianism... I think of Henry Dreyfuss, who designed almost everything we handle today. I met him in London in '69 and he told me: "It's all over, I'm going to retire and take a trip around the world. With all the hope we've invested in design, I don't understand how chaos still keeps on developing." He wanted to travel around the world to find out what was "going wrong." What tranquil naiveté! Dreyfuss going out on his own to look for the causes, like an investigator. Now that's the contrary of utopia!

Paradoxically, I was quite an admirer of Quasar's dandyism.[24] He had a good communication strategy. I liked his approach: he said that everything was getting lighter, ideas as well as things.

Experimentation

Research is endless, it always heads toward the unknown, always trampling through fields that haven't been sufficiently explored, or have been explored with too many preconceived

[24] Quasar (Nguyen Mahn Khan: engineer of the Ponts et Chaussée school and furniture designer, born in 1934 in Hanoi.

ideas. So I don't see how the idea of research for the sake of research would be a concept in itself. Here the perspective is one of blazing a path toward the future. I'm an enemy of utopia because it has often involuntarily contributed to barbarism. People project lost illusions onto the past, while continuing the attempt to fabricate worlds that have no reasonable chance of being any better. Design is research in the absolute sense of the word: it works on the existing, the possible, and the probable. What's concrete is to do a critique of what exists: it's implacable, it's beneath the microscope, you dissect it. There's today for the existing, tomorrow or even next week for the possible, and next year for the probable. You don't look too far ahead: I don't even say the next decade, I say next year. I don't want to talk about the middle and long term, because developments are enclosed in such a system of constraints that if you are able to effect even small bits of progress it's very gratifying.

With respect to this analysis, the possible inquires into everything that could change in order for things to become still better. Let me take an example from the subjects I give my students: "Take a few recent, dateable inventions, and try to see at what time the elements necessary to reveal them were available." The result is that there are many inventions that could have been carried out much earlier in history. Here's the proof that the barrier to innovation is cultural, moral, linked to economics, to religion, and to routine!

The probable has nothing to do with what people read in the tea leaves—prediction is for those who are horrified by uncertainty. It's more a matter of asking, with great openness of mind, what are things likely to evolve toward, that is, after the elimination of all the illusions and impossible or unbelievable hypotheses. That's the moment where you can eliminate. So the probable takes on its full meaning in relation to the existing, the possible and the future.

Politics

When Jean Baudrillard and I left for America,[25] I assured him he wasn't required to be provocative... He answered: "What do you think? I don't have a political sex!" I'd answer the same thing. If politics is being useful, from my point of view I distinguish between being an artist and being a designer. I'm not only in the service of a client, but in the service of people in general. In my case, politics means that I often go beyond the commission by putting myself in the place of the commissioner. If he is deficient, then I take his place, and if his project is limited, I propose going further. That's the real role of the designer, and that's political!

After '68, everything was politicized, everything was deconstructed. As soon as you begin doubting the basis of the society you live in, it's certain that you damage it. But is that really a problem? As soon as people start saying "in France," I get suspicious, because for me, that doesn't exist. The field in which I operate isn't France, and I'm not particularly interested in what's happening in Romarantin! Outside the country I visit design centers which are very active, not only on the contemporary level, but also for what happened yesterday. A Wagenfeld museum just opened in Bremen.

[25] Meeting of the ICSID in Aspen, where Roger Tallon led the French delegation (1970).

Palladium, crystal glasses
Ed. Arnolfo di Cambio, 1999

Marylin, crystal glasses
Ed. Arnolfo di Cambio, 1999

Bacchus, crystal glasses
Ed. Arnolfo di Cambio, 1999

Ligne Aphrodite, crystal glasses
Ed. Arnolfo di Cambio, 1999

Wunderbar! Because here, we're far from having a museum dedicated to Prouvé.[26] So I don't think design much interests the French, who are nonetheless full of passion for cars, hi-fi, Internet... They are materially in the present, but not in the ideas that make the present.

Incursions

Art

I worked with César and also with Yves Klein—above all, I worked concretely with them. It was similar to my experimental extrapolations in scenography, where I left behind the usual field of the designer in his agency with his products, to go into large organizations. I always loved the big productions, like Montréal[27] or Osaka...[28]

In the late fifties I met Yves Klein, a modernist in his way. He was someone rather vulnerable whom I tried to protect from whatever might perturb his approach. He didn't work with artists but with architects or designers, because he needed information and trustworthy people who could put him into touch with industrialists. He was looking for experts to work with him on his scale models.

[26] Jean Prouvé, French engineer, builder, architect, and creator of furniture (1901-1984).
[27] ICSID meeting (cf. note 8) in Montréal, as part of the World Exhibition of 1967. Roger Tallon worked on the education pavilion.
[28] For the World Exhibition in Osaka in 1970, Roger Tallon was named stage director and coordinator of the French pavilion.

I think we're not destined to be one single thing. Where I'm concerned, either I worked for myself as an artist and tried to participate in more or less concrete events, or I did design. And when I decided to take that second road, I abandoned all the rest. Being a designer meant working with industry and trying to avoid the ambiguities. Today, some people think you can be both at once: yes, you can be both, but I think it's too ambiguous. Even if the fact of working for others on products that one wouldn't necessarily use oneself can appear very sterile. The sole compensation for that is to go over to the other side of creativity, the kind I would call free, open creativity, above all with people who are seeking something new (not academics or crowd pleasers). Klein's approach was absolutely different from the artists of our time. When he put his fingers on something concrete, it was always for abstract reasons: he was in the contrary of what I practiced. So I materialized his projects because he was changing our culture. Another way of approaching the relations with the material universe.

With César it was very different. We were involved concretely, working together on his materials and the way they could be used: he did his experiments and I did utilitarian things. I followed someone who was close to me culturally, and he had this will to go beyond the current formalism. For him, art was fixated there. His fixed idea was recuperation, and I showed him new products, like heat-formed plastics, foam plastics. I did lots of projects for him.

For me, art exists only as a terrain of adventures, an escape hatch, a place where you can go off wandering, and where I put in my own effort by working in research groups. What interests me is living art, art that is in the process of being made, and that is capable of breaking through the ice cap of forms. Not like the people who go to the museum on Sunday: they admire the cleverness of a given artist, but they don't go any further, because they have no idea of the innovation that it represents for a particular epoch. So art augments my possibilities and takes me away from concentration on the little problems. It also engenders pathologies and maniacal, repetitive behavior. And that's not good for design. I preferred to remain in the role of designer, even if at one moment I almost slipped over into art. But I find it frightening, the idea that something I make would then become me. That's what kept me from being an artist. And I wouldn't have had the same success. Today, for example, it's much more difficult to break into design than when I started. There isn't much to shake up or overcome.

Media

I read a lot and I try to explore all the layers. I buy 400 francs worth of journals every week. Some are always in the pile and then I skip around through other fields… Sometimes these magazines are addressed to such a narrow interest that it's almost an overdose.

When Catherine Millet founded *Art Press* in '72, the magazine was above all addressed to people who liked extremes… That job took on a double meaning for me: I wanted to help Catherine construct her magazine, and I wanted to give rise to an object halfway between a book and a research tool. The journal, by comparison to the book, is a particular point in history. The newspaper is "hot": continuous and event-oriented, lots of deeds and dates, but few interpretations. The book is "cold": it works retrospectively. Whereas the journal or magazine is "lukewarm" and contains both event and interpretation. The layout of *Art Press* is debatable, but I had good reason to establish a consistent calibration. The typographical range is narrow, as in a book: there is voluntarily little gradation in the titles. That has to do with one of the great preoccupations of designers in the sixties, who often did their typography in Helvetica, a simple, modest alphabet. I remember Roland Barthes being furious at seeing his name no larger than that of an insignificant little writer no one mentions any more today. My desire for no typographical hierarchization was in order not to be manipulated by the hierarchy of the titles. So I did a journal where Catherine could control at once the content and the form, where she wouldn't be at the mercy of some uninspired graphic designer. Since then, *Art Press* has absorbed all the changes linked to more than twenty-five years of activity, but the general line has remained almost the same.

Architecture

Having never set limits on my work, I'm not paralyzed by the fact of not having any architectural legitimacy. At the French railway company I fiddled with almost everything, even the uniforms. A good experience. The only thing that I was unfortunately unable to deal with was the architecture of the stations, which also comes from the origins of the railroad. Today there's no coherence between these spaces and the train, because the architects struggle against unity, without any concern for legibility.

"Portrait-screens"
Visual reconstitution of Ingres'
Napoleon on Canova, galerie de
France, Paris 1965

In 1970 I did a counter-project for the French pavilion in Osaka. Like the others at the time, it was planned to be an inflatable structure, but the chosen architect didn't know the technologies and wasn't able to perfect them. The general commissioner then decided to cut short the damage, get rid of the architect and do a "solid" pavilion. So I did a project for surface animation. At the beginning, just for honor's sake, I'd had quite an advanced project, which was rejected by the decision-makers. It was a very informal proposal, with hard foam poured over a metal skeleton: I was told it would be impossible to have De Gaulle enter "that thing" for the inauguration.

On the question of the object as structure, I think of Oldenburg who "gigantified" objects in the form of sculptures. So why not do buildings like Starck's in Tokyo? The motive force is the scale. From my point of view, architecture should remain an approach that deals with the totality of a utilitarian space, not a dazzling symbolic exercise.

Fashion

Everything you create emerges in a given environment. But fashion can't be a basis, because it's ephemeral. There is sartorial fashion and furniture fashion, which are placed in the category of styles. I tried to avoid that to the extent that what I was doing was not for private use. Even my furniture, which is often used in private, was conceived for public spaces: it was tough and it met the safety standards. So I don't see how someone living in a certain time can do durable things that fit current fashion. Except by leaving an imprint on the period, that is, giving it the character of fashion; but for me that represents a fleeting sociological effect. At the time when Téléavia came out, for example, it wasn't in fashion, it was contemporary. The designer doesn't have to do durable things, because what he does is technologically destined to go out of date. He marks his time in a precise way, and he has to be of his time. *Clockwork Orange* was of its time, whereas *2001, A Space Odyssey* was futuristic. Olivier Mourge[29] was able to translate the approach of Panton[30] and make it a "consumer item for future consumption."

I consider Verner Panton to be the great man of our time, a veritable researcher who wanted to discover signs for the future and to pull free of tradition. He dabbled in everything, without preconceived aesthetic ideas: in fact, that's what he was reproached for. He even pushed things to a kind of extreme by designing some real kitsch. But if you look at his work from a professional angle, everything Panton did was original: he was at the leading edge... One of his great strengths was to make maximum use of the possibilities offered by the new materials, applied to original structures. His work was considered as going beyond the period, and today we realize that he still doesn't fit among what I call the "bourgeois slums" of the seventh arrondissement in Paris. They're still gasping under all that fake Louis XV!

[29] Olivier Mourgue, French designer born in 1939, chosen in 1968 by the director Stanley Kubrick who selected the lounge chair "Djinn" as a decorative element for his film *2001, A Space Odyssey.*
[30] Verner Panton: Danish architect and designer (1926-1998).

Colour pictures index

1: *Chrono Pyramidion*, for the beginning of the third millenium, 1999
Ed.: Christofle

2 & 6: Two covers for *Art Press* n°245, 1999 & n°239, 1999

3/4/5: Automat Group, 3 views of the exhibition at Zanini gallery, Paris, 1970

7: César and Roger Tallon behind a *Portrait-chair* made in the image of César
(conceived in 1967 for the Orly Airport crib), 1993

8: Helicoïd stairs, 1966
aluminium, for the Galerie Lacloche (view in the gallery)

9/10: Folding chairs *TS*, 1978
Wood, Ed.: Sentou

11: *Méridienne*, in collaboration with César, 1970
Ed.: Mobilier National

12/14: *Cryptogamme*, pouffe (aluminium and stuffing), 1969-1970
Ed.: Mobilier National

13: *Cryptogammes* and *Téléavia* TV set

15: Hommage to André Citroën, project of Roadster,
(computer image) DEIS 1997

16: Reticulated map for the RER net in Paris, 1976

17: Chronometer for Lip, 1973

18/19: *Météor* (new regional train in Paris), 1997

20: Montmartre Funicular for the RATP (Paris), 1991

21: *Matra–Metro 208*, Lille-Toulouse-Rennes, 1999

23: Project of GNER in collaboration with M. Vignelli (GB)

24: *Eurostar* project for the SNCF, 1994

25: Texas-TGV, for GEC Alsthom- Bombardier, 1993

26: TGV (interior), for ADSA

27: Taiwan-TGV project, for Siemens Alsthom, 1998

28: TGV Sony Playstation, at the occasion of the Football World Cup, 1998

29: Bar of the Atlantique-TGV for SNCF, 1989

30: The beach, new pilot study for the Seguin island in Paris, 1999

31: Design Labor, Bremerhaven, *Alligator programme*, 1996

32: Design Labor, Bremerhaven, *Alligator programme*, 1996

33: Project of a pylon for EDF (France), 1994

34: Space rocket, collaboration with Yves Klein, 1961

2 ▶

3/ 4/ 5 ▶

6 ▶

◄ 7

◄ 8

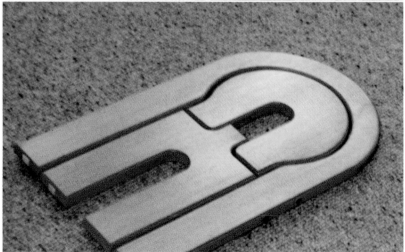

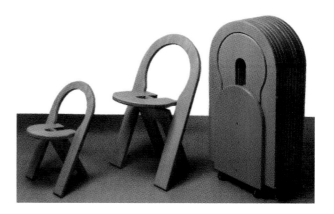

11 ►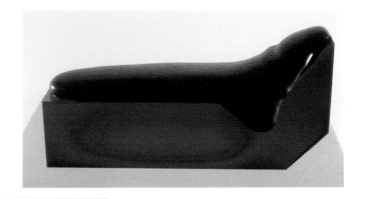

12/ 13 ►

14 ►

15 ◀

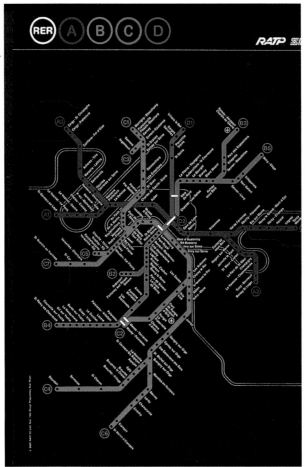

◄ 18

◄ 19

20 ▶

21 ▶

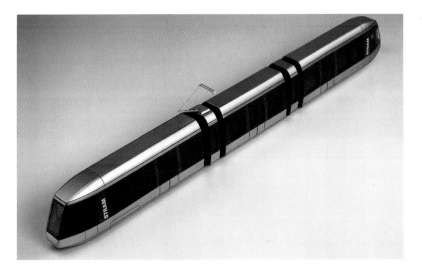

24 ▶

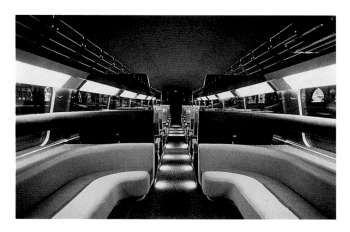

25 ▶

26 ▶

◄ 27

◄ 28

◄ 29

30 ►

31 ▼

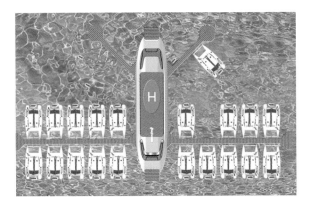

32 ►

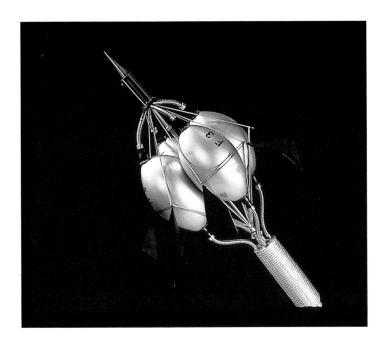

Biography

1929
Born in Paris

1944-50
engineering studies

1951
In charge of Graphic communication for Caterpillar-France
Consultant for Du Pont de Nemours' european subsidiaries

1953
Meets Jacques Viénot and joins Technès, office for technical and æsthetic studies founded in 1949 (with Jean Parthenay)
Takes part in the preparation of the International Congress of Industrial Æsthetic, where the creation of the ICSID was decided (the International Council of Societies of Industrial Design the first congress of which was organised in 1957 in Paris)

1957
Teaches industrial design at the Ecole des Arts Appliqués (first design lecture in France)

1963
Creates with Jacques Dumont the Design section of the ENSAD (Ecole Nationale Supérieure des Arts Décoratifs) in Paris

1964
Member of the Study Group Education of the ICSID, Bruges seminar (Belgium)

1965
Designs the first "Portrait Screens" (*Écran-Portraits*)

1966
Develops his researches on projections on volumes
Registers a patent for the *Électroncéphale*
Experiments the "talking heads" (*Têtes Parlantes*)

1967
Joins the group *Automat*
Study Group Education seminar at Syracuse University (United States)

1968

Founds the teachers group *001* which elaborates–with Claude Cobbi–the first project of the Institut de l'Environnement (Environment Institute)

Member of the ICSID-UNESCO delegation (with Sir Misha Black) at the INTI Buenos Aires colloquium

1969

ICSID's congress in London

Expert at the Haut Comité de l'Environnement (Environment High Comity)

1970

Travels to Nadodka (Vladivostok)-Moscow with the Transsiberian. Visits the VNITE (Youri Soloviev-Larissa Jadova), meets Constantin Simonov and some opponent creators

Leads the French delegation at the Aspen congress (United-States)

Writes the "Centro Colombia", a study for the Foreign Trade Center of Colombia

1971

ICSID's congress in Vienna

Study Group's seminar at Ulm (Germany)

1973

Founds his agency: Design Programmes (in join venture with Sofinova, run by Christian Marbach)

Nominated honorary member of the Faculty of Royal Designers for Industry of the Royal Society of Arts (Great-Britain)

1975

Eurocom (Jacques Douce, Havas group) becomes the first partner of Design Programmes

1979

Innov Elf becomes partner of Design Programmes and Jean-François Boissel closely participates to its development

1984

Formation of ADSA + partners with Pierre Paulin, Michel Schreiber and Roger Tallon (in association with Marc Lebailly)

1985

"Grand Prix national de la création industrielle" granted by the Ministère de la Culture

1992

Granted "Commandeur des Arts et des Lettres"

1993

Exhibition of Roger Tallon, "Itinéraire d'un designer industriel", Centre Georges Pompidou, Paris

1994

Fusion Eurocam/RSCGl Schreiber and Roger Tallon
Formation of Euro RSCG design, by the fusion ADSA/SOPHA

1995/1996

Takes part in the researches and formation in the Institute Design Labor of Bremerhaven (Germany)

1997/1998

Takes part in the weekly chronicle "Journal de la Création" of Serge Moatti on the TV channel la "Cinq"

1999

Takes part in the exhibition "Interni"–"Milan, Capital of Design"

Studies, Projects and Product Design (selection)

(the dates correspond to the beginning of the studies, which can sometimes last for several years)

1954
- Universal milling machine *2N* for Gambin
- *Duplex*, 9,5 mm camera and *Monaco*, double-size projector for Pathé (label Beauté France 1956 and Gold Medal at the Milan Triennial in 1957)
- *Brandt-Luxe B600*, sewing machine for Sodame
- *Micox*, electric drill for Gendron

1955
- *Micro 3*, Project of a fuel-efficient mini-car for Peugeot
- Range of fork-lift trucks for Salev
- *Europ*, 8 or 9,5 mm projector and *Lido*, 9,5 mm camera for Pathé (label Beauté France 1956 and Gold medal at the Milan Triennial in 1957)
- *Taon*, 125 cm3 compact motocycle for Derny-Motors

1956
- Automatic washing machine for Sauter

1957
- Airport truck 193 (Orly/Air France) for Fenwick
- *Véronic*, camera for Sem
- Lathes *Gallic 16* and *Gallic 14* for la Mondiale (Belgium) - awarded Signe d'Or

1958
- Range of fork-lift trucks for Fenwick
- Logo and image of Fenwick Aviation (helicopters Bell)
- Domestic appliances for Peugeot (coffee mill, domestic appliances, electrical toothbrush…)
- Range of fridges and washing machine for Frigidaire
- Tape recorder for Polydict
- *Japy Style*, typewriter for Japy
- Range of adhesive tape holders for Rubafix and conception of a new brand image for Rubafix
- *Vincennes,* map designing machine for Uvex, Machines department of Frigiali
- *Didacton*, study of a new concept of material for professionnal teaching - fitting and automation- for La Mondiale (Belgium)

1959
- *Celtic*, range of lathes and *Viking,* milling machine, for La Mondiale (Belgium)
- Televisions for Téléavia, subsidiary company of Sud-Aviation, (specially an adjustable set with an aluminium feet and a tinted screen)

1960
- *Super Caravelle,* fridge, 315 lit. with transparent window for Frigeavia
- *Automatic-Dishwasher-Giravia* for Frigeavia
- *Santa Maria*, study and model for the fitting-out of *the Super Caravelle*, for Sud-Aviation, Toulouse
- Radio sets for Thomson
- Electric shaver (licence Braun) for Thomson
- *Wimpy,* seats (moulded plywood and aluminium) for Sentou
- *Focamatic,* photo camera and electronic microscope for OPL
- Microscope for Nachet

1962
-Office furnitures for Flambo
- Film reader of the bubble chamber CERN (Geneva) for Som-Berthiot

1963
- *Japy Message*, portable typewriter and electric typewriter *S 29* for Japy
- Portable TV set *P 111* for Téléavia

1964
- Range of electric drills for Peugeot
- Design of the CIFOM stand (Information center on moulded casting); creation of the helicoid stairs, the seats and tables of the *M 400* line to come. Ipoustéguy creates a sculpture for the occasion (*Ecbatane*)

1966
- Seats and stools of the *M 400* serie for the galerie Lacloche
- Edition of the helicoid stairs in aluminium by the galerie Lacloche
- *Orlymatic*, *Orly Club*, *Orly Super,* office seats for Flambo
- Serie of office accessories for Buysse
- *URSS*, electric locomotive for Alsthom

1967
- Mexico subway for CIMT
- First project and model of the TGV 001 for Alsthom
- First fast computer printer for Benson

- *3T* line (porcelain crockery by Raynaud, stainless steel cutlery by Ravinet d'Enfert, crystal glasses by Daum); distributed by Sola France
- "Zombies- chairs", for the new café *L'Astrolabe*, boulevard Saint-Germain in Paris (the café was designed and realised by Maurice Marty)
- Competition for the new Ford Capri in collaboration with Ets. Chausson
- Transparencies projector for Kodak
- *Didac 800*, analyser machine for Intertechnique
- *Urba 2000*, study of an experimental vehicle on air-cushion for Maurice Barthalon

1968
- Electro-erosion machine for Stokvis (USSR)
- *La Bulle*, project and prototype of compact-car for the urban traffic flow, for RDEB (Belgium)

1969
- *Cryptogamme*, a furniture line created for the Mobilier national, for the cafeteria of the Grand Palais in Paris
- *Top Avia*, stacking TV set system for Téléavia

1970
- *Cosmos*, a range of switches and power points for Gardy (Belgium)

1971
- Global program of design for the Corail train of the SNCF in collaboration with Mariane Persine Heissler and Alain Baillon

1972
- Graphic design of the new art magazine Art Press created by Catherine Millet
- *Pin Spot*, lighting system for Erco (Germany)

1973
- Winner of the competition for a new telephone, for France Télécom
- Range of plastic oil cans for Elf
- *Mach 2000*, a new range of watches for Lip

1974
- New brand image for the european pool of sleepers TEN, for the UIC (Union Internationale des chemins de fer)
- Ski boots for Salomon
- *Solid Sound System*, hi-fi system for Cineco (Shure)
- *Super Corail*, project (two levels) for the SNCF
- *Fluoryl*, tooth-brushes for Fluocaril (in collaboration with Monika Jost)

1975
- Project and model for the fitting up of the South-East TGV for the SNCF
- Sun oil bottles, accessories and PLV for Bergasol

1976
- Project for the subway in Caracas - image, signage system, material - for the Société Franco-Belge
- General study for the new RER (Parisian regional trains) - system's logic, logo, signage system, map, furniture, equipment…- in collaboration with Massimo Vignelli, Rudi Meyer, Peter Keller, Henri-Pierre Jeudy
- *Urbus,* project of bus for a competition organised by the Ministère des Transports
- *Mini-Max,* project of decomposable mini-car presented at the Batell Institut of Geneva

1977
- Pilot study for signage system of railway stations and re-organisation of Austerlits railway station in Paris
- *TMX,* project of a multifunction mini-vehicle for Ets Marden

1978
- *Bultop,* rubber pavement with semi-spheric chips, for Dunlop/Protecmo
- Stacking chairs *TS* for Sentou Galerie
- *Chêne Tramé,* modular system to enhance the value of second choice wood, for Gilor, under the aegis of the ONF (Forest National Office)

1979
- *Medius,* office seats system for Eurosit
- *Smach System*- creation and elaboration of a brand new ball sport

1980
- *Twin 550 CNC,* manufacturing system with computer controls for la Mondiale (Belgium)
- Author of a general report on the introduction of electronic directories in french homes
- *Minitel,* invention of the name and model of set for Télécom
- *Bank,* cooking and food conservation compartment for Cidelcem
- *SM 11,* car radio for Blaupunkt (Germany)

1982
- *Goupil,* computer system and brand image for SMT

- Range of watches for Certina (Suisse)
- *Goupils III*, new generation of computers for SMT
- Brand image for electronic publishing and computers for Nathan and Thomson, and creation of the brands *TO7* and *VIFI,* Nathan
- Project of glasses frame system for American Optical (United States)
- Institutional image and signage system for the Centre d'Études des Systèmes et des Techniques Avancées (CESTA) of the Ministère de la Recherche

1983
- New concept of glasses frame for Essilor
- Graphic image, signage system, furniture and uniforms for the Conservatoire National du Littoral
- Design of the TGV Atlantique for the SNCF
- New uniforms for the ticket inspectors of the SNCF in collaboration with Michel Schreiber
- Project of a 600m high "Tower of the Liberties", to make of Paris the international headquarters of Human Rights, at the occasion of the commemoration of the bicentenary of the French Revolution

1984
- *Situ*, information points for the RATP
- Ski glasses for Cébé

1985
- *Infostop*, information system at the bus stops for the RATP
- New logo, new graphic image, and standards guide for the SNCF (in collaboration with Yanka Neuman)
- Global study for a new image of French currency (coins and bills), under the aegis of the Ministère de la Culture, and presented to the Banque de France
- Project of a new system of registration plates in order to personalize the regions (in collaboration with Rémy Deroche)
- Competition for the project SPNV 2000 (subway and regional train) for the DB (Germany)

1986
- Development of the TGV Atlantique project

1987
- Winner of the competition for the fitting up and the design of the *Eurostar TGV* for the BR (Great Britain), the SNCB (Belgium) and the SNCF

- New graphic image of the promotionnal publishings and the fitting up of the offices of the SIRPA, Ministère de la Défense

1991
- Montmartre Funicular for the RATP: vehicles (and stations in collaboration with François Deslaugiers, architect)
- *Météor*, subway for the RATP
- *Méga TGV* (two levels) in collaboration with François Lacôte and Louis-Marie Cléon for the SNCF, and with Michel Poisson for GEC Alsthom (in collaboration with Hugues Fruchard)

1992
- New *Val 208* for Matra
- Toulouse Subway - image, signage system and ground architecture (in collaboration with the architect Paul Lamarque and the designer Wilfried Delebecque)
- Project of a subway for Rennes - image, signage system and ground architecture
- Programme Eurotunnel - design management of the commercial image, signage system and design of the shuttle (in collaboration with Dominique Pierzo), Wolf Ollins associés

1993
- Project of the north-american TGV (Texas and Canada, GEC Alsthom - Bombardier constructors)
- VR (National railways of Finland) - new image, logo, signage system and design of the TGV
- Mosgortrans/RATP - new image, signage system, design and fitting up of Moscow busses

1994
- Competition for a system of interior links for Roissy Airport- in association with Poma Gasky

1995
- *Muse*, project of a hight way tunnel in the western parisian area in collaboration with Bouygues
- *TGV des mers*, pre- project in collaboration with Marc Lebrun Alsthom St Nazaire

1996/1997
- *The Alligator's Project* –system of naval constructions standardized by Yatchs

from 40 to 80 meters in collaboration with the Institute Design Leber Bremerhaven
- Pre-project for the development of the DASA aerospace communication centre in
Bremme with the Institut Design Leber Bremerhaven
- Research on a new distribution module of domestic gas, Total Gaz
- *Hommage à Jean Citroën,* Research on a concept-car with Pascal Cacninacci-
DEIS

1998
- Renewal programme for the South East TVG
-Making of a promotional Playstation TGV for Sony

1999
-Chrono–pyramidion, third millenium silver trophee for Christofle
- *The Beach*, pre-project for the re-planning of the Seguin island
- New image, new equipping of the subway in Marseille

Exhibitions and Events

1962

Collaborates with Yves Klein and César for the exhibition "Antagonismes 2, l'objet" at the Musée des Arts Décoratifs, Paris

1963

Psychedelic projections on the habitable sculpture by André Bloc at Meudon (reception for the closure of the ICSID congress in Paris)

1965

Takes part in the exhibition "La Main" at the galerie Claude Bernard and presentation of *Le Poing* with projection of images

1966

Participation to the exhibition "L'Objet 2" at the galerie Lacloche (shows the *Lit Métamorphique*)

1967

Organises with Jean-Jacques Lebel the Festival of Free Expression in Saint-Tropez

ICSID congress in Montreal during the World Fair. Collaborates to the Education Pavilion

Participates to the "crib" by César at the Orly airport, presenting the *Portrait-chairs*

1969

Inaugural exhibition of the CCI (Industrial Creation Center) "Qu'est-ce que le Design?" - Colombo, Eames, Eichler, Panton, Tallon

1970

Scenography and coordination of the programme of the French Pavilion at the Osaka World Fair (Mitsubichi constructor)

Shows the *Giant Talking Heads* (Françoise Hardy, Sylvie Vartan, Georges Moustaki) at the French Pavilion of Osaka

"Modern Chairs 1918-1970", exhibition in London

1971

"Le Design Français", exhibition at the CCI, Paris

1981

"Paris-Paris 1937-1957", exhibition at the Georges Pompidou Center, Paris

1984

"Mobilier National, 20 ans de création", exhibition at the CCI/Centre Georges Pompidou, Paris

1986

"Les Années Plastiques", exhibition at the Cité des Sciences et de l'Industrie de La Villette, Paris

1988

"Design français 1960-1990, trois décennies", exhibition at the CCI/Centre Georges Pompidou/APCI, Paris

1991

"Caravelle 2", exhibition at the 2nd International Quadriennal of Design, Lyon, 1991

1993

"Design, miroir du siècle", exhibition, at the Grand Palais, Paris

"Roger Tallon, itinéraire d'un designer industriel", exhibition organised by the Mnam-CCI

Bibliography (selection)

Essays by Roger Tallon

"Petits ou grands dessins du stylisme industriel", *Architecture 55* (Belgium), n°14, 1955

"Arts ménagers et néomachinisme", *Esthétique industrielle*, n°60, 1963

"Propos sur la pratique du design et sur son avenir en France", *L'Architecture d'Aujourd'hui*, n°155, April-May 1971

"Le Cadre de vie contemporain", *Maison et Jardin*, n°183, May 1972

Tallon, R., Jeudy, H.-P., "Signalisation, signalétique, la différence?", *Communication et langage*, n°36, December 1977

"Le Design est un évènement humain, en rupture avec la reconduite de la tradition", *La Revue Parlementaire*, May 1983

"Dix mesures fondamentales à prendre", *La Revue Parlementaire*, July 1983

"Le Système TGV présente sa troisième génération: le maxi TGV ou TGV 2N", *Au Bonheur des formes. Design français 1945-1992*, Paris, Ed. du Regard, 1992

Books

Huisman, Denis, Patrix Georges, *L'Esthétique industrielle*, Paris, PUF, coll. "Que-sais-je?", 1961

Lavrillier, Marc, *50 Designers dal 1950 al 1975*, Novara, Ed. Görlich, 1978

Qu'est-ce que le design?, exhibition catalogue, Centre de Création Industrielle/CCI (Center for Industrial Creation), Paris, 1969

Modern Chairs 1918-1970, exhibition catalogue, London, 1970

Le Design Français, catalogue of the exhibition, Centre de Création Industrielle/CCI, 1971

Garner, Philippe, *Twentieth Century Furniture*, London, Phaidon, 1980

Millet, Catherine, "Un designer à Paris", *in: Paris-Paris 1937-1957*, exhibition catalogue, Centre Georges Pompidou, Paris, Ed. du Centre Georges Pompidou, 1981

Hiesinger, Kathryn B., Marcus, Georges H., *Design since 1945*, New York, Philadelphia Museum of Art, Rizzoli, 1983

Mobilier National, 20 ans de création, exhibition catalogue, CCI/Centre Georges Pompidou, Paris, Éd. du Centre Georges Pompidou, 1984

Morgan, Alan Lee, *Contemporary designers*, London, Chicago, St. James press, 1985

Les Années Plastiques, exhibition catalogue, Cité des Sciences et de l'Industrie de La Villette, Paris, Ed. Alternatives, 1986

Design français 1960-1990, trois décennies, exhibition catalogue, CCI/Centre Georges Pompidou/APCI, Paris, Ed. du Centre Georges Pompidou, 1988

Polieri, J., *Scénographie, théâtre, cinéma, télévision*, Paris, Ed. Jean-Michel Place, 1990

Caravelle 2, exhibition catalogue, Second international quadriennal of Design, Lyon, 1991

Design, miroir du siècle, exhibition catalogue, Grand Palais, Paris, Flammarion/APCI, 1993

Also available from Dis Voir

ÉDITIONS DIS VOIR:
3, RUE BEAUTREILLIS—F-75004 PARIS
PHONE (33/1) 48 87 07 09
FAX (33/1) 48 87 07 14
EMAIL: DISVOIR@AOL.COM